Books by Daphne Rose Kingma

Coming Apart

Heart & Soul

The Men We Never Knew

True Love

Weddings from the Heart

Finding True Love

To Have and to Hold

A Lifetime of Love

The Future of Love

The 9 Types of Lovers

The Book of Love

365
Days of Love

DAPHNE ROSE KINGMA

CONARI PRESS
Berkeley, California

Conari Press books are distributed by Publishers Group West.

This book was previously published under the title *A Garland of Love.*

Cover design: Lisa Buckley
Cover illustration: Susan Jokelson
Cover photography: Lace © Image Club
Book design: Suzanne Albertson

ISBN: 1-57324-759-6

This has been previously cataloged by the
Library of Congress under this title

Kingma, Daphne Rose.
A garland of love : daily reflections on the magic
and meaning of love / Daphne Rose Kingma.
p.   cm.
ISBN: 0-943233-27-5
1. Love. 2. Intimacy (Psychology).
3. Interpersonal communication. I. Title

BF575.L8K4966 1992

152.4'1-dc20   91-39816

Printed in Canada.

02 03   TC   10 9 8 7 6 5 4 3 2

Through love are we born;

With love shall we live;

To love we shall return.

INTRODUCTION

*T*hree hundred and sixty-five days of love—whether or not you've said that to yourself, that's probably the amount of love you'd like to have. And yet you may not know how to get it—or what it will look like when it arrives.

It's easy to forget that, in fact, love comes in many forms. It's not just the passionate excitement of a new romance. It is, just as wonderfully, a friendship of forty years rekindled after decades of separation, the flash of delight in your grandchildren's eyes, deathbed words of reconciliation with a parent or ex-partner, the sweetness of shared community, of differences worked through over years of seasons with your wife or husband.

We usually experience love in "a relationship," with one or several persons; a sweetheart or spouse, siblings, family, a circle of friends. And it is through all these connections that we have an opportunity to grow, to see how our own natures engage with those of others. In relationships we are invited to expand, to change, to become more aware, more generous, more loving. To that end, this book is a teaching on some of the steps toward awareness and awakening.

At the heart of all of these relationships, of course, lies our ability to know and love ourselves, to discover and heal the emotional wounds that have shaped us and affected our talent for loving. For that reason, some of the days' meditations are focused on the practice of self-love.

Discovering the gifts and limits of your capacity for loving others is also terribly important. We tend to be acquainted with our own need to be loved, to be held, heard, understood, chosen, and cherished; but we are not nearly as aware of our great need to be loving. Yet it is through our own capacity *to love*, to create the experience of connection we so long for, that we discover the circle of love to be completed and fulfilled.

For love isn't just the luscious feelings we have after a fabulous first date; it is the energy of the universe. It is the silver thread that weaves us all, human beings and creatures alike, into a single shimmering cloth. And it is our awareness of the mystery and the beauty of this energy, and of its omnipresence, that gives us a sense of connection to the All, and bathes our spirits in a wash of deep joy.

Our human steps on the path to this joy are exquisitely simple and, at times, frustratingly complex. And so I offer this book of days as a companion on your path, and send it to you with my love.

Daphne Rose Kingma

It's Happening Now

*W*hatever you dream of, hope for, want to change, or wish would happen in your life—it's happening now. Wanting change, dreaming a dream, wishing for things to become as you envision them to be, are all acts of the unconscious that, molecule by molecule, set in motion the chemistry of change.

Imagination is instantaneous; achieving what we hope for takes time. Still, once we have started to hold a vision—in our hearts and minds, in the feelings of hope and expectation that we quietly acknowledge to ourselves—we have already initiated the process that can make the possibility real.

So whatever you desire, whatever change you want to occur, whatever outcome you seek, remember that it's happening now. The desire itself is already creating the outcome.

Healing Fears

*L*oving someone brings up old fears: the fear that things will be the same as they were in the past, the fear that the person you love now will make the same mistakes you lived through before, the fear that, having revealed yourself, the person who loves you won't care enough to learn who you really are, let alone minister to your needs.

We all have fears, and we can either silently coddle them—and ensure that they'll come true—or reveal them and allow the person who loves us to love us in the midst of them and beyond.

Healing old fears takes time. The only thing that can help you overcome your fears is more time . . . and more love.

Infused with Love

*A*ny virtue, attribute, or aptitude of personality will come to its full power only when it is bound together with love. No talent in its own right and no quality of character will reach the apogee of its impact until we marry it in our hearts to the love that will alchemize it to its full potential.

For love confers a quality of truth upon everything into which it is infused, a presence of light that elevates it far beyond the ordinary, lifts it to the place where we can hear the deepest meanings that are trying to be spoken, see with eyes beyond eyes the truth of the invisible, the mystery of the unseen.

Therefore, whatever your form of expression, whether it be language, music, color and design, or the movement of your body, be sure you fill it with love, so it can be received to the depths of its power.

Receiving Feelings

*B*eing able to receive another person's feelings is a sign of emotional maturity. That's because as difficult as it may be to express what you yourself feel, it is even more difficult to allow the expression of another person's feelings to penetrate the crust of your own self-involvement.

A sign of the quality of your relationship and of your own emotional capabilities is the ability to truly take in another person's emotional content.

Reach for this capacity today; allow the person you love to touch you, move you, even to enrage you, for receiving another person's feelings is the measure of the maturity of your love.

Honoring Your Spirit

S piritual abuse is the subtlest form of unlove that we know. It means that in the most sensitive avenue of our being, the place in us that is connected with the deepest truths of the universe, we are treated like idiots or morons, told we don't know what we know, don't feel what we feel. Instead of having our spiritual gifts acknowledged by those around us, we have our precious perceptions negated when they occur.

Because, in general, we don't take account of our spirits, we are often also unaware of how deeply they have been bruised and mistreated. The healing for a hurt and wounded spirit is the love with which you honor it yourself. So begin now to honor your beautiful spirit by trusting what you see, feel, and know.

The Mother of Your Friends

*T*o the mother of each of your friends you owe a great debt. These are the women who gave birth to the people with whom you share the pleasures of life. The consequences of their nurturing—and even of their failures—are what you have now to treasure and enjoy through all the days of your friendships.

So today, find a way to express your appreciation for the love that has been passed on to you because of the mothers of your friends. Send a card or note, or, when the opportunity arises, tell them directly how grateful you feel. Something like: "Thank you for bringing _____ into the world and for all that you did to help her become the friend that I cherish. I want you to know how much I appreciate and enjoy her, how very grateful I am to you for being her wonderful mother."

The Gifted Lover

*F*rom time to time we are given the gift of a wonderful lover, a person whose special grace brings us into the physical presence of the holy. Because of his or her beautifully developed sensuality, we are reminded that sexual passion is one of the most precious pleasures of being alive.

If you have been given the gift of a wonderful lover, allow yourself to receive it. Acknowledge the power of sexual healing to change you, to make you more beautifully whole. And give thanks to the person whose capacity to love you as a body allows you to encounter a new depth of loving with your soul.

Love As Duty

*L*ove doesn't always consist of doing what we "feel like" doing. Love is also a duty, what we have chosen to do because we have made a commitment to loving.

Dutiful love demands that we move beyond the impulse of momentary sensation and reach for what love calls upon us to do, rather than just how it makes us feel.

Thus we not only love our children because they delight us, we love—and discipline—them in order that they may grow up to be whole human beings. We love our parents not because they loved us perfectly, but because we have made a commitment to honor them for the places they hold in our history. We love our friends through a fiery argument because we have made a commitment to be steadfast in our friendship; and we love ourselves even when we are disappointed in our own behavior, because as a spiritual duty we have made a commitment to honor ourselves.

Making Peace with Your Body

*M*aking peace with your body, accepting it as it is, nurturing it with your care, feeding it well, strengthening it with exercise, admiring its beautiful aspects, honoring it with comfortable clothes, treating it as a temple, enjoying it as a ballroom, being awed by it as a palace—all these are expressions of healthy physical self-honoring.

Being at peace with your body isn't easy. It takes effort. At the most complex level it means coming to terms with the fact that your body both *is* and *is not* your essence. Therefore, making peace with it is a paradox. You must nurture it as though it will last forever—at the same time knowing that it will break down and that, at the end of your life, you will finally have to abandon it.

Living with this paradox is a challenging spiritual lesson, but living it out in awareness is the highest kind of love you can give to your miraculous body.

Emotional Hide and Seek

When you don't express your feelings directly, in a sense you make emotional servants out of the people around you. Instead of taking a risk and being clear—asking for what you need, saying what you feel—you manipulate others through silence, sickness, absence, or moodiness into trying to figure out how to love you.

The inability or unwillingness to express your feelings is a form of emotional tyranny and not a way of maintaining privacy as you may think.

Risking self-revelation is an act of vulnerability that always fosters the deepening of any relationship. So don't be an emotional scaredy-cat. Say what you feel today and strengthen the bonds of your love by taking the risk of revealing yourself.

An Absence of Strangers

*E*very human being is your counterpart. Every other human being possesses and embodies aspects of yourself: your dreams, your sorrows, your hope that your life will not turn out to be a dirty joke.

For each one of us there was a time when the world was young, a springtime of spirit that was tested by the winters of discontent, and in the midst of each of our lives lies the haunting shadow of death. Therefore we are all quite alike; indeed at the core we are all one—all lost and found in the same mysterious enterprise that is life.

Hold this truth in your heart as you go about your day, and the world will cease to be inhabited by strangers. The journey of life will no longer be a process of loneliness. Indeed you will find a kindred soul in everyone you meet.

The Meaning of Family

*T*he members of your family were given to you to help shape you. You may not always love them. They may not always understand you. In fact, your most important experience of them may come when, because of your differences, you separate from them. But they are your teachers and sculptors. Their influences, more than almost any other in your lifetime, formed you.

If you have parents, brothers, and sisters who share your life's pleasures and sorrows, who, comfortably, you enjoy; be thankful for them. But if your family members are people whose lifestyles and values diverge so painfully far from your own that you feel like a stranger among them, give thanks for them too. For in the crucible of their inability to understand you they have defined you, insisted that you discover most deeply who you are, forced you, without their even quite intending to, into your truest and most beautiful becoming.

A Process in Time

*T*hose whom we have wounded may be able to forgive us only sometime in the future. Just because you feel better now that you've screamed and raved about whatever it was that scared you, doesn't mean that your darling, the dartboard for your outpourings, will have recovered from your hysterical attack the minute that you're done with it.

Forgiveness is a process in time, the time it takes to understand the deeper motivations of the person who was mindlessly cruel, the time it takes for new experiences to be applied like soft gauze bandages over scraped hearts and bruised feelings. You may want forgiveness now; be ready to return to a state of balance, but that can't always happen according to your own sense of timing.

Therefore, if you have wounded someone and desire forgiveness—a return to the way things were before the bad thing happened—you must not only apologize, but also have patience. Forgiveness takes time.

Your One and Only

*Y*our body is the cocoon for your soul. It is you. Whatever you do in your life will be expressed through it in one way or another. It is a material construction of the rarest components, of the most elegant capacities.

Therefore, its well-being is of infinite importance. Everything you dream of for your life is posited on having your health. So love yourself by taking care of your one and only beautiful and precious body.

The Grace of Gratitude

Gratitude is an act of grace, a way of blessing yourself into a future abundance of gifts. For when you are grateful you open a channel of receiving in yourself. You develop the sense that what you have already been given, you can be given again.

In relation to others, gratitude is good manners; in relation to ourselves, it is a habit of the heart and a spiritual discipline. For when we are grateful, we expect the cosmos to bless us.

What specific things in your life do you have to be thankful for today? By making a list of them, you can be consciously grateful. And gratitude is the way to make blessings happen again.

They Weren't There for Me

O ften when people are mad at their parents they'll say, "they weren't there for me." When people say this they are usually referring to some vague pain, not to the specific disappointment they felt with one or another parent.

She wasn't there after school, waiting with cookies and milk? He wasn't at home at all? He wouldn't talk to you? She didn't tuck you in bed or read you stories at bedtime?

We say our parents "weren't there" because we don't want to feel a particular pain or our fear that the future will consist of others who won't "be there" for us. In order not to repeat the past, we need to specifically identify our pain so that now, in the present that contains the possibility of being loved, we can ask for what we want and notice that, more than we ever imagined, we can and we do receive it.

Behavior Has Consequences

*B*ehavior has consequences. They may not be noticeable or immediate, but in time they will make themselves inescapably clear. If you drink to excess now the consequences of your habit may not be visible for ten or twenty years; but in time you will see them. If you offer the gift of healing love now, the rewards of your gift likewise may not be apparent for decades.

But make no mistake, what you do will bear fruit. And whether that fruit is a poison apple that will bring your life to an untimely close or a rare exotic flower that will open your awareness to worlds beyond worlds, know this: whatever you are doing now will surely have a result.

Therefore undertake your words and actions with conscious awareness, knowing that what they are now is only the merest seedling of what, in time, they will become.

Relinquishing Control

*L*etting go of the reins—of life, of the person you love, of the way you think things ought to be—allows you to open to the possibility of love.

Relinquishing control is an act of faith and of supreme liberation. For the love that comes into view when you do this is real love—not love as you thought, imagined, or expected, not love according to your plan, but the kind of love that, unasked for and unruly as a rainstorm or a wild animal, seizes you by the heart and makes you whole again.

This is the love that will teach you, change you, and shape you, the love which in being so big and asking so much, will show you who you are and what you came here to do.

Where do you need to let go of the reins? In what circumstances can you surrender control? How can you open the door to real love?

The Joy of Love

*A*bove all, love is to be enjoyed. I often hear people talk about "working on" their relationships or on any one of a dozen issues within them, as if their relationships were only difficult—mechanical, problematic, pieces of machinery perennially breaking down and needing non-stop repair.

A relationship does take effort, and we have to be willing to do the required work. But we also need to remember that love is above all a pleasure, a treasure to delight in, a miracle to savor, a gift to be enjoyed.

Today, don't "work on" your love. Abandon all effort and allow it just to be.

For No Reason Whatsoever

*L*ove isn't based on merit; it's a gift from the angels. No matter how much we may try to be worthy of it or insist it into our lives—by preparing ourselves, by being in the right place, by trying to be deserving—love when it comes is a purely gratuitous gift, an unexpected miracle.

You do need to do all you can to entice love to knock on your door, but at the same time you need to remember that when it arrives it has come both because of and despite everything you have done.

Love appears for no reason whatsoever—and for every reason. It's a favor from the angels, not a consequence of effort.

The Power of Proximity

*T*hrough a process of almost mystical osmosis, proximity generates transformation. We experience another person's essence through the possibilities we see ourselves enacting just because of being close to them. There are certain ways we change only and precisely because of being in another person's presence.

For this reason, we need to choose the persons with whom we surround ourselves with the utmost care—whose breath we breathe, whose sleep we dream, whose words we hear—knowing that in time and through proximity we will, inevitably, take on the colorations of their character.

To see those who share the intimate space of your life in this light is to see them differently. Whose intimate presence fills you with peace? With play? With joy?

The Ultimate Connection

*L*ove is what connects us to the spiritual. This is the deepest reason we seek it. We don't always consciously know this. We imagine we want love because it distracts and delights us, but actually we look for it because it meets us at the level of our most profound longing.

After we have tried to satisfy ourselves in all the ways we do, with diversions and achievements, we eventually return to the aching inner yearning for the real thing: the love that liberates us from the endless little and big disappointments of our lives, the love that delivers us to the life of the spirit, which only and always can truly fill our hearts.

JANUARY 23

Who Deserves Love?

*L*oving yourself means that of all the people you see, know, and recognize to be in need of your special love and attention, you put yourself near the top of the list.

This means that you don't always think first or only of the other person but that you also consider what you need and want: he needs time to play golf, but I need some quiet time with him; the kids need new shoes, but I'm going to go nuts if I can't get a haircut.

Sometimes you'll get your way; other times you'll forgo your preference. Loving yourself does not mean doing only what you want; it just means that you also consider yourself.

Beyond Blaming

E motional maturity is that developmental state of grace in which you have transcended the concept so familiar to three-year-olds and other young souls—of blaming someone or everyone else for what happens in your life—and have started to take responsibility for your own behavior.

For most of us, developing emotional maturity is a process. It requires knowing yourself—what pushes your buttons and why—as well as a certain degree of complexity of perception. What this means is that you are able to turn a situation around in your mind and look at it from a different point of view: maybe she didn't respond to me because she's a self-centered jerk or maybe she didn't respond because she's going through some pain of her own.

The more you step beyond the simplemindedness of blame, the more you will step into emotional maturity—and the pleasures of a far more intricate perception of yourself and others.

Not Like You

*T*he person you love won't look at love or your relationship in exactly the same way you do. He or she
may have very different feelings about how it should be
conducted, how you should argue, how and when to make
love—even what your relationship means.

For your darling, the most important thing about loving
you may be that you're there, every day, every night to come
home to; while for you the specific kinds of attention you
receive—sweet words and flowers, anniversary presents—
may mean more than anything else. You may handle crises
in totally different ways: he may go to the gym to work out;
you may talk on the phone for hours with your best friend.

Understanding that your beloved may not feel the same
way—and in some sense may not even occupy the same relationship as you do—is one of the greatest opportunities for
growth in any intimate relationship.

Moving On

A relationship has been completed and emotional recovery is well under way when the person you once loved no longer has the capacity to pull your little heartstrings, make you angry, or reduce you to tears.

This state of emotional resolution doesn't mean that you never loved the person with whom you were once involved. It means that you have resolved your feelings, that your emotional blackboard is clear, and that now, expectantly, you can wait for a different hand to lift a fresh piece of chalk and write you new messages of love and endearment.

If you still have strong feelings about a relationship you need to let go of, allow your heart to open to it one more time. Express your resentments, perhaps in writing; then also write your appreciations. And then set your feelings aside and move on.

Becoming Yourself

We all have so much to go through in order to become ourselves. We have to understand our histories and childhoods; to rage in our hearts at our parents and then forgive them; to heal our emotional wounds, honor our talents, acknowledge our feelings and give voice to them; explore and succeed at relationships; discover our work, accept our finitude, and do what we came here to do.

In a sense we never completely "become ourselves." We are always in the process of becoming. But in order to have a sense of the beauty of the process, invite yourself today to consider exactly where you are in your journey. What have you already accomplished? Where are you headed? What are you still waiting for? Look at your path with compassion for the process of becoming yourself is a lifelong enterprise.

Finding Your Strength

*E*ventually in the process of your self-healing, you will find your own strength. Through the careful hand-holding of your own spirit, through recognizing, honoring, and expressing your feelings, by nurturing your body as the vessel that holds your spirit in the web of life, you will discover that you have, without your consciously knowing it, developed the inner sturdiness from which you can function on your own behalf.

This interior growth is a miracle of intimate compassion, a seedling of loving yourself that will bloom, in time, into the capacity for truly loving others.

So today acknowledge the strength that is yours. If you're still not sure that you're strong, make a list of all your little strengths so that, as the day goes on, you can consciously treasure the strength that you have already attained.

Lives Have Themes

*E*ach of our lives is a meditation on a particular tragic theme: betrayal and abandonment, sexual or spiritual violation, the insult of incarnation as expressed in conflicts with the body, or the uses and abuses of power, to name but a few. Whatever the theme in your life, it is both your personal sorrow and the source of the greatest contributions you can make to others.

Life is full of people who have turned their wounds into opportunities: the sensitive child mocked for his insight who becomes a therapist; the woman blinded in a car accident caused by a drunk teenager who becomes a high-school drug and alcohol counselor. When we embrace our tragedies they become the blueprint for what we, uniquely, can offer the world.

What is the tragic theme in your life? And what are the special gifts that are the consequence of it? How do you hope to share these gifts with the world?

Forever Yours

*Y*ou never really lose anybody you have loved. No matter what may separate you—time, distance, the relationships that preceded or may follow this one, even death—the love you shared and the soul you encountered through that love is yours forever in your heart.

Every person you have loved has changed you. What you have become because of loving them is how they will be with you always. A relationship may come to an end. But love is eternal. You will never lose anyone whom you have truly loved.

You Are the Gift

*N*othing is more precious than the rare, exquisite, and utterly unrepeatable essence that is you. When you offer yourself to another human being—by revealing yourself, by disclosing your fears and dreams, the losses that have shaped and transformed you—you give the greatest gift that you can, the gift of your unique essence.

Far from being selfish, true self-disclosure is a miracle of intimacy, for in revealing your tender, intricate inner self, you invite the person to whom you are speaking not only to see who you are, but also to see himself.

To whom would you like to reveal yourself?

Seeking Sustenance

*F*inding sustenance for our spirit runs against the grain of what is commonly available to us. We are offered possessions, distractions, and entertainments which, rather than taking us to a deeper level of ourselves, endlessly tease us with shallowness. Rather than being invited to discover how strongly we feel, how much we can be moved by life, we are constantly talked out of living our depth.

Therefore seeking sustenance for our spirits—in art, in conversation, in entertainment, in what we buy and how we spend our time—has become not something we can do easily, but something that requires effort, something we must undertake as a spiritual enterprise.

To open your heart, to feel more, to sense the meaning of life, to experience your own depth—make it your business today to seek the sustenance that will truly nourish your spirit.

To Want Love

*T*o want love is to want God. To want light. To want peace. To want joy. To want Love.

Today, allow yourself to really want the love you really want.

Love as Devotion

*L*ove, should we choose to live it at the level of devotion, is far more than simply riding the waves of our emotions, which come and go with the ever-changing tides of our experience. Love as devotion—approaching the person we love with openness, pure-hearted gratitude, and holy recognition—is one of the purest forms of love, for it serves the beloved with love and in return it asks for nothing.

In love as devotion our lives become an expression of the belief that love itself is the highest gift we can offer. When we occupy the state of heart and mind that is love, our lives become an expression of that love, and we remember that more than anything else that we have, do, achieve, or desire, our love is of value. When we make an offering of that love to another human being, this, in itself, is an act of devotion.

Love's Paradox

W hen we are endeavoring to love ourselves, to come into our power, the greatest challenge is being humble. To know that you have limits and are not a god is the starting point of recognizing your strengths.

What are the limits you need to face? What is the compassion you need to give yourself about them? Can you be comfortable now, inhabiting your humility, knowing that in time it will become one of your most powerful attributes?

The Season of Our Discontent

*D*iscontent is the seed of change, so when you encounter it in yourself, don't be disheartened. It's an announcement, from you to yourself, that things as they are aren't good enough for you, that you deserve better, that you intend to instigate a change.

Capitalizing on discontent, however, takes courage and effort. You need to see what your discomfort is saying or else, like a dog chasing its tail, you'll just keep going around and around, drawing endless meaningless circles.

What is your discontent of the moment, and what is it saying to you? With what part of your life are you currently dissatisfied? What single step can you take today to ensure that the seed of your discontent will blossom, in time, into change?

No Special Indemnity

*J*ust because you love somebody doesn't mean you can't hurt them—and by the same token it doesn't give you the right to hurt them. In fact, proximity deepens the exquisiteness of the pain we can cause one another. Because we're attached, we can hurt each other more.

Therefore be mindful of the power to wound that intimacy creates. Don't feel as though you can do no wrong. Be careful how you speak and move. Handle the person you cherish most with goose-down feathers and soft kid gloves.

The Beauty of Example

*N*othing can teach your children more about love than the example of the love you share with your child's other parent. In the family configuration, it is the relationship between the parents that is primary, not the relationship between any one child and a parent. It is, in fact, these so-called "special" relationships between certain children and their parents that often amount to abuse for a child and signify the breakdown of the relationship between the two primary adults.

It is important to tell, show, and embody the fact that you love your wife or husband in a way that is categorically different from how you love your children. This will reveal the bond of love that you have secured with your marriage, and it will stand as the beautiful example your children can follow for their whole lives.

Your Need for Love

*D*on't be ashamed of your need for love and don't be afraid to express it: "I need you to choose me"; "I need you to stand by me and to comfort me always"; "I need you to love me because I need so much to be loved."

The revelation of your need for love is a gift, an invitation to love that the person who truly loves you will feel the greatest joy in fulfilling.

The Gift of Life

*T*o receive the gift of life and of this world, with all its mysteries and magic, its trials, travails, and limitations, is the love of the creature for the creator and our thanksgiving for being given the gift of life.

Loving all other creatures—the stars, the trees, the animals and people with whom we share life—is the way we extend the love that created the world. Through love we enhance and affirm the miracle of our being.

Love is our song of thanksgiving for living, our gladness that we were invited to be here, our celebration of being alive.

Getting Through Hard Times

*I*t's easy to love when we're blissfully happy, when we are in love and everything is running smoothly. But love is tested in hard times, developed in crisis, and reaches its full maturity when unexpected tragedies befall.

So although we neither seek, nor should we ever welcome, tragedy, we need to remember that there is always a hidden jewel stitched into the hem of its garment. Hard times invite the enlargement of the love in us, as, stretched beyond our limits, we find that our love expands.

The Tyranny of Manipulation

*M*anipulation is the antithesis of love. It is the wily psychological domination of one person's being, feelings, and intentions by another, the erasure of one person's essence through another person's assault.

Manipulation is getting another person to do what you want them to do without acknowledging your need to have them do it, a wiping away of another person's priorities in favor of your own. When you manipulate you treat yourself as though your needs, desires, and hopes are unworthy of being fulfilled (or else you would ask for them directly), and you treat the person you are manipulating as though, aside from what you want him or her to do for you, he or she is valueless.

Don't manipulate. Begin today to value yourself and the people you love by daring to ask directly for what you need.

The Interface

*M*aking love is the interface of the physical and the spiritual, the mortal and the immortal. Making love brings everything together. Making love is the balm and the bond, the giving and the gift.

Elevating Our Relationships

*U*ntil our relationships evolve to the point that they express true love and spiritual freedom, they will be cages of convention for the suppression of our capacity for love.

The spiritual evolution of intimate relationships includes not only the expansion of our capacity for loving one another, but also sharing our love and power with others and finding the form in which to share our love and power with the world.

Today commit yourself to embracing the spiritual evolution that your intimate relationships invite. Ask them—and yourself—to be more than you ever imagined, to seek, find, and become love itself.

How's Your Love Life?

*T*o the question, "How's your love life?" we should always be able to answer: "My love is boundless; my life is full."

To the extent that we cannot, we are living within limits that were long ago imposed on us. Instead of being jubilant and daring, seeing the love that surrounds us, allowing ourselves to tease more love into being, we play victim and accept impoverishment as a given.

Today, on the day that celebrates love, acknowledge the love, whatever its form, that surrounds you. Don't wait for the Valentine; become one. Be the embodiment of the "I love you" that will generate an "I love you" in return!

The Baby and the Bathwater

*D*on't undermine your relationship by endlessly focusing on its imperfections. Every relationship has flaws and always will. They are the punctuation, the counterpoint to what makes it the sanctuary it is; but don't give them too much credit or airtime. We come to feel about things the way we speak of them.

So speak lovingly about your relationship; honor its joys and pleasures, the benefaction of its uniqueness, the mystery of its existence. Then, rather than being a project that you will have to constantly work at, it will become a miracle that you can endlessly enjoy.

Tendrils of Mortality

*N*ow and again we have experiences that make us aware of how fine is the thread that connects us to our delicate mortality. Someone we love is suddenly, unexpectedly wounded. The ladder falls, our finger is cut and bleeds madly, the oncoming car swerves mindlessly, crashing head-on into our own and we see how fragile we are.

When disaster strikes someone you love dearly, or an out-of-the-blue experience awakens your sense of mortality and the possibility of loss, the question isn't how can you learn to detach, to feel less, so you won't have to deal with the anguish of potential bereavement, but, how can you live every moment being more deeply grateful that you have had an opportunity to love at all.

What Do You Want?

*K*nowing what you want to receive from love is the precondition of getting it. If love is only a vague idea, a miracle you keep hoping will happen, chances are the love that could fill up your heart and transform your life will not be forthcoming for you.

The love we can receive is very specific; it is never a random inappropriate enterprise. So, if you really do want love, take some time right now to discover exactly what you want it to look like and feel like. What words do you want the person who loves you to say to you? What kind of happy times you want to share with her or him?

Make a list and then keep its contents in mind. If you don't, the love you get will be a fuzzy random response to an equally vague request and not the love that fulfills your wildest—and most pedestrian—dreams.

Love Is Not Enough

*J*ust because you love somebody doesn't mean you will know how to make that person feel loved. Love is a state of being, a feeling in the heart, but to generate that same feeling in the heart of another human being is a process of relationship. Unlike love, which is a gift, a relationship—the experience of being in emotional union with another person—is developed through the behaviors and experiences we create in the presence of the person about whom we feel love.

Because of this, everything you do or say, fail to do or neglect to say, to the person you love, has in itself the capacity to deepen or lessen the quality of your bond, and in the end, to either destroy or beautifully develop your relationship.

Today remember the power your behavior has to shape the quality of your relationship.

More Than We Are

*L*ove calls us into being as the highest expressions of ourselves, makes us servants and saints, confessors and healers. When we love, we have no choice but to enlarge our definition of ourselves. Because of love we become not only more than we were but more than we ever intended to be.

What do you think you would see if you invited love to call out the best in you? How would you stretch? What would be the highest expression of you as yourself?

The Elegance of Forgiveness

W hen we forgive another human being we don't erase the terrible thing he has done; but in the face of his willingness to acknowledge the hurt he has caused us, we receive him again and differently, with his flaws and his perfection, into the state of grace that is our wholehearted acceptance.

In fact, the beauty of forgiveness is that it is neither blind nor dumb. Forgetting is not forgiving, but mere mental lassitude; ignoring is not forgiving, but an amputation of your own capacities for perception. Forgiveness sees the wound, can remember it if need be, is willing to work through the pain of it, and, through the alchemy of forgiveness, is willing to start over.

Who do you need to forgive? What are the words you need to say—in your heart or directly to the person—so that you can begin again.

The Way to Get Loved

We don't get loved out of the blue, by chance, or for no reason at all. We get loved because we need love, and the way to get loved is to ask.

There's an old joke about a man who stands on a street corner and asks every passer-by for fifty dollars. When an observer makes fun of him for standing around all day and making a fool of himself, the man says, "I may look ridiculous, but I'll bet I get a lot more fifty-dollar bills than you do."

So it is with love. We get the love we ask for. We may not get it from everyone or all the time; but we get a lot more when we take the risk of asking for it than if we stand on the street corner speechless, wishing and hoping that somehow it will just show up. Take the risk of asking for love today.

Taking Out the Trash

*A*nger is like garbage: the longer you keep it around the worse it stinks. Suppressed, outdated anger can do more than almost anything else to upset the equilibrium of an otherwise good relationship. Therefore it behooves you—for the sweetness of your own soul and for the well-being of your relationship—to express whatever anger you have as quickly and concisely as you can.

So today, figure out what you're angry about. Find the words that most clearly express it; and then report it to the person it should be directed to. That way you can have the fragrance of fine perfume instead of the smell of rotting garbage in your emotional living room.

Love, the Elusive

*L*ove is a gift. We cannot insist it into being. It will not simply respond to our longings, our desperation, or our pleas.

Love comes in its own good time, when we ask for it and when we least expect it, for no reason and for every reason, in response to our pleading and in spite of our unreadiness. The only thing we can do is know that we want to be loved. Create the need, and by the hands of the angels, it will be filled.

Today, allow yourself to feel your need for love.

No Meaningless Moments

*E*very interaction in a relationship leads either toward or away from intimacy. No behavior is neutral. With everything you do and say, with the texture and intention of every word, action, or gesture, you are ever so delicately sculpting the structure of your relationship.

The tone of your voice invites your partner closer or, imperceptibly, encourages her to move away. The way you look or don't look at him when he speaks or when you are making love will draw you deeper into the bond of love or encourage the gradual dissolution of that bond.

Nothing you do lacks meaning; everything you do has the power, on a most intricate level, to build or, stone by stone, dismantle, the cathedral of your relationship.

Your Inspiring Example

*L*oving yourself is always also a gift to the person who loves you. Loving and taking care of yourself shows that, at your depth, you value the gift of life and, in particular, your own life.

Honoring yourself with kindness and self-nurturing, tenderly caring for your body, your mind, and your infinitely delicate spirit, is a way of inspiring your beloved to take care of himself or herself, too.

The Real Thing

*N*othing will make you happier or make you feel more like yourself than a true, disclosing, emotional exchange with another human being. Nothing is more wonderful than being able to tell someone else who you are, to open your heart, reveal your true colors, and engage with another person at the level of your own refinement.

Today, step across whatever shyness or fears you may have about showing yourself, and allow yourself, with someone you trust, to make the small—or immense—disclosure that for a long time you have wanted to make.

What an incredible joy it will be to be present as yourself!

More to Come

*T*o imagine that you have already arrived, that you are already completely yourself, that there is nothing more to discover, no more to go through, is to live your life unconsciously, to miss out on the pleasures and lessons of life. It is, in fact, to miss out on life itself.

If, without quite intending to, you have been living this static, swamplike semblance of a life, ask yourself right now what you're missing, or, more important, what you would feel you had missed, if this were the last day of your life.

And then start doing something about it right this minute!

Your Children's Keeper

*A*ll our adult relationships are incarnations of the unloved child in search of the love that he or she didn't get. We are all trying to be seen, heard, cherished, valued, and known.

Therefore, if you have children, love them well. They have no one to love them but you; and the love you fail to give them is the love they will have to spend the rest of their lives attempting to recover.

And if you don't have children, be very tender and kind to the unloved child in yourself. You can begin the process by acknowledging that he exists, that she is still waiting for love. In what special ways can you honor this unloved child? What is this precious child still in need of?

Timetable of Miracles

*R*eally wonderful things don't happen definitively; they happen gradually.

We often look for the dramatic turning point, the *shaza-am* that will move our life instantly in another direction. But this is rarely the case. Most of us don't win the lottery or become rock stars overnight. Instead, our lives are a gradual and subtle process of unfolding, an ever-so-delicate movement that sets our path in a different direction.

If you've been impatient about the movement in your life, remind yourself that without your consciously noticing, a great many things have already changed. What path that you dreamed of long ago do you now find yourself on? What things that you hoped for long ago have already occurred? Today allow yourself to acknowledge the gradual advent of miracles in your life.

Expanding Your Love

*A*llowing the person you love to have significant relationships with people besides yourself, to love, support, and nurture others, is taking your love to a higher plane, extending it into the spiritual dimension.

In allowing your husband to console your best friend, in letting your wife encourage your brother, in permitting your children to go on vacations with the family down the street, in sharing your dentist, your masseur, your minister with someone you know who could benefit from their healing expertise, you expand the reach and range of your love.

This sharing and opening of our relationships goes against the grain of our internal myth of possessiveness, that we own and control those whom we love. But controlling and possessing are the antithesis of love. Although there is risk when we share, there is also incredible joy in letting those around us partake in the gift of love that has already been given to us.

Response Is Participation

Sometimes we think of love only as the things we ourselves do, think, say, or perform. The truth is that in any loving encounter, response is also a powerful form of participation. In fact, a response that makes it clear that you have heard, felt, seen, or been changed by what has been said or done by another person is one of the greatest gifts of connection you can offer in any relationship.

We all need to know that who we are and what we do have impact. Response is the way we learn that we are important and that what we do has had an effect. Response is one of the sculpting forces of love.

Distraction of Possessions

*P*ossessions can never do for us the things that people can. Things, no matter how grand, wonderful, or impressive, can never fill the place in our hearts that longs for real love. Things can distract us, impress us, detain us, give us bogus status, and momentarily cheer us up; but they can never take the place in our souls of the love of a single compassionate human being.

Do you allow your possessions or the time it takes you to acquire them or maintain them to keep you from the truly soul-nourishing experience of being loved? If you do, consider what spirit-enhancing practice you might incorporate into your life. Meditation, prayer, community service—all of these in time will allow you to deliver yourself from the tyranny of possessions.

The Miracle of Empathy

*E*mpathy is truly one of love's miracles. In empathy we not only feel sorry for, but we feel *with* another person. This is much more than simply looking at her situation, feeling bad that she's in it, and wishing it would go away. Empathy is powerful. And active.

In empathy we ask ourselves to enter into the experience of others, to feel their sorrow, know their pain, experience their fear. Empathy is a very accomplished practice because it requires that we ourselves have felt first, that we have not shied away from our own sorrow, pain, or fear.

Empathy connects us very deeply to others. For in a sense we go inside their feeling selves, that most private of places, and there give them company. Empathy is a spiritual undertaking, for in its capacity to connect us so deeply to one another, it is truly the end of divisiveness, the beginning of our sense of union.

The Emotional Spectrum

When you suppress feelings at one end of the emotional spectrum, you inevitably suppress feelings at the other end as well. Conversely, when you allow the vividness of your emotional self to shine in any part of the spectrum, you invite it to blossom in all the others.

So if you want to feel fully alive and emotionally vibrant, you must be willing to feel not only your delight and joy, your tenderness and passion, but also your fear, anger, disappointment, and loss.

Be daring enough to live with the full range of your emotions. Don't miss the exhilaration of your joy because you're afraid of feeling the pinch of your sorrow.

Invisible Competition

*O*ne of the best-kept secrets about the parent-child relationship is that on an unconscious level it has a built-in element of competition. Parents are resentful that simply by virtue of their age, children have life, time, opportunities, and experiences available to them that have already passed by their parents.

How parents consciously and unconsciously acknowledge this inherent competition, and how they treat their children with regard to it, is a measure of their capacity to love. How children respond to the expressed and unexpressed competition of their parents will be a measure of how, in time, they will be able to love their own children in return.

Honor your children by squarely facing the competitiveness you may feel about them.

Don't Consider the Source

*T*he origin of friendship is magic, as unpredictable as the rabbit produced from the magician's hat. Friendships sprout up in unlikely places: two women meet at a birthday party for a man they both dated and hated; roommates at a conference, whose housekeeping habits drove each other crazy, discover they have a dozen other things in common; a man meets his ex-wife's best friend at the gym and finds out that, along with lifting weights they are both engaged in a similar process of emotional healing.

However it arrives, no matter how ridiculously or unexpectedly it may commence, a friendship is a treasure, truly a bit of magic, a gratuitous rabbit in the top hat of our lives.

Believe in Love

*T*he greatest act of faith is to believe in love: to believe that you'll fall in love when you haven't been loved for years; to consider that love will heal your childhood wounds; to know that you are worthy of being loved; to conclude that you can love and that your love will be valued and received; to assume that love can last; to trust that love really can change the world.

Since all of us have been betrayed to the depths of our souls, to believe in love at all is an act of spirit based not on experience, but on pure faith. Believing in love is difficult; but when we are able to make this exquisite, extravagant leap, the faith we have will create the love we desire.

Believe, believe in love!

A Pearl of Great Price

What we cherish is costly—the beautiful watch was expensive, the vacation took six years of savings to pay for, the time to write required getting up early.

So, too, with the loves that shape us and change us. We pay for them with our time, with the commitments we can't make to other people, with our parents' or children's disapproval, with our vocational or geographic choices.

Today, take a little time to assess what you've paid for your love. Make a list of all the things, people, resources, and opportunities you've given up in order to have it. Then cherish it all the more, for the price you have paid for your love will have revealed its true value.

Inner Knowing

*H*aving a sense of yourself, an "identity" or "self-concept" as the psychologists say, is one of the greatest gifts of having been loved. When we know who we are—what we're about as individuals, what moves and touches us, what we're afraid of, what hurts, what abilities and limitations we have—we are in possession of that rarest of favors, a blueprint of ourselves.

This inner knowing, this capacity to enjoy, experience, discover, explore, and continue to create yourself, is one of the greatest benedictions of parental love. If you have received it, be grateful. If it is yours as a parent to give, be aware that to the child who receives it, it will be a lifetime treasure. For there is no greater possession than truly knowing yourself.

A Reflection of Honor

*I*t should be an honor to see yourself in your beloved's eyes.

To see in the person who loves you the excellence that resides in yourself, the best that you are, the highest that you can reach for, the most that you can aspire to, is a reflection we should all hope to attain.

This means that rather than being lazy, assuming that you will always be loved just as you are, for no reason (and taking for granted the good opinion your sweetheart has of you), you will always strive to embody our highest ideals. You will stretch. You will reach to become even more than you are now, so that in the eyes of the person who loves you, you will always see pride, amazement, honor, delight, and joy.

Love Test

Sometimes our real feelings about love are all but invisible to us. Things stand in our way but we don't know what they are; we have secret hopes about love but we don't permit ourselves to know them. We have misconceptions about how love should be but we never bring them to consciousness.

Here's a little love test to help you discover a few of your unconscious notions about love:

For me to be loved would be _____.

For me to know I am worthy of being loved would be _____.

For me to become more loving would require me to _____.

For me to become more able to receive love would require me to _____.

In Consideration

Consideration is being able to imagine how what you say or do will affect another person. It isn't a passing shallow form of etiquette, but rather the profound recognition that the other person isn't you. It reflects your desire to honor that other person with respect to his or her own feelings, circumstances, needs, and limitations.

Consideration is holding the needs of another in just as high a regard as your own, and, on whatever occasion, whatever your particular agenda, taking into account that the other person is also a part of what's happening.

Consideration asks us to step, at least for a minute, outside ourselves. To become more considerate, start inquiring: How are you? What do you need? Is this all right for you? Is there anything else I can do? Consideration is down-home compassion. Consideration breeds consideration ... for you too.

Receiving the Light

W hen someone you love has died, she will bestow her light on you from wherever she is. The attributes, genius, and talents that were his will come to inhabit you in a strange, mysterious way; his absence will fill you with his presence.

In the midst of your loss, this is his legacy. This is her gift. Wait for it. Look for it. Expect it. And surely you will receive it.

To Open Our Hearts

S o many of our hearts are battered or closed because of the almost unbearable wounds we received from our fathers and mothers, our thoughtlessly cruel siblings, unconscious strangers and friends.

To open our hearts, to love and to be able to be loved, means that we must revisit the wound, walk once again on the troubled ground, so that with a heart made strong by the scarring, we can open again.

Today press yourself beyond the constriction of your wounding and beg yourself to open again—no matter what you must go back and look at, no matter how long the journey.

Really Being Seen

We feel loved when we feel seen, deeply perceived, apprehended, and responded to by another human being. Being able to be seen requires vulnerability. It means that we reveal ourselves—or that we put ourselves in such close proximity to another human being that he or she can really see us.

Some of us are afraid of being seen. We don't want our secrets to show. We're afraid that, having disclosed the inner reaches of ourselves, we won't feel safe or get loved. Others of us are afraid of not being seen, of remaining forever invisible and unacknowledged.

Today, reveal something to the person you love which, in the past, you have kept hidden. Then allow yourself to see something in her which, previously, you overlooked or ignored. Intimacy grows when we are seen, when we allow ourselves to truly behold one another.

Allow yourself to be seen.

Beyond the Boundaries

*T*here are certain experiences—running, dancing, making love, listening to music, reading scintillating prose—that take us out beyond the boundaries between the flesh and spirit.

When we are in this pure, undifferentiated state of being, separated not even from our selves, we are in the state of love.

Clowning Around

Of all the happy attributes you can bring to a relationship, humor is one of the most delicious. Telling a joke, good-naturedly enjoying one another's foibles and eccentricities, laughing together at how life has turned out, is good aspirin for any small passing emotional pain in any tending-to-be-too-serious relationship.

So connect with the clown in yourself. Take a look at your life and see where, invariably, you get strung out on being serious. Then try a little humor, a good or even a lousy joke.

Lighten up!

The Blessing of Silence

*T*here is no more special gift you can give yourself than an experience of silence and solitude—time out of time, time for contemplation, time to step out of the ordinary, time to move beyond your limits into the quiet place.

We are motivated, and life as we know it instructs us, to keep ourselves occupied, to work, to do, to accomplish, to be constantly endlessly active. In doing so, we accomplish so much that we actually start believing that achievement is everything. We miss the complexities that lie beneath the surface, the deep mysterious peace, the God in each of us.

Be still and see yourself today as part of the eye of God.

The Common Thread

We're sometimes afraid of strangers, of unfamiliar others because they are different. We don't know how they are like us; we don't know how we are like them.

When we feel this fear, we tend to withdraw and close down and at times miss out on what could be a wonderful experience. How many friends do you have, for example, who upon first acquaintance seemed irritating, or odd, or so unlike you that if they hadn't made the first gesture you would never have gotten to know them?

When we're afraid it's because we've lost or haven't yet found the common thread, that which at the center is alike in all of us: that we are human, that we suffer, that we change, that we die.

Take a risk today with someone you encounter; and try to discover the common thread.

Love Is the Measure

*L*ove is the archtype, the measure of all our other experiences. Whatever moves us or captures our attention, we compare it at some level to our experience of love. "It's like falling in love"; "Why it's almost like being in love," we say; "My life would be perfect, if only I were in love."

Whether or not we are consciously aware of it, we continually make these comparisons. Love is the benchmark against which we measure all the other aspects of our lives, for, in our souls, we know that love is the supreme experience.

What Lies In Store

*T*he tragedies that may befall us—difficulties with our children, the anguishing watch we may have to keep as our parents' capabilities diminish, illnesses out of the blue—all these will ask us to expand.

We may feel unprepared for these crises, and indeed we are unprepared for them. But as they unfold they will show us not only our capacity to grow, but also our ability to love.

Therefore, although we all tend to hope that life will be simple, that things will stay as they are, we also need to welcome the changes of life—of growth, of loss, of altered circumstances. For these are the crises that build our souls, that enlarge our true capacity for love.

Right now, ask yourself for the grace that will allow you not only to weather the crises that besiege your life but also to view them as occasions for heart-shaping transformations.

Our True Possession

*T*ime is the one commodity above all others that is our true possession. Objects come and go, relationships enter and recede, jobs change and circumstances alter, but time is a constant. We have it to do with whatever we choose.

We often overlook the use of our time: when we sleep we are passing time; when we have a conversation with a dear friend we are sharing time; when we nurture a suffering other we are giving of our time; when we have a mindless argument we are wasting time.

Time's most important quality is that it passes, that we have only a finite amount of it. Therefore, be aware of its value and know that when you give it, share it, or waste it, you are spending the most precious commodity that you possess. When we give our time we are giving of our life.

Many Splendored

A relationship can express itself on many levels: on the physical level as making love, on the emotional level as feeling love, on the spiritual level as being love.

To have a relationship on only the physical level is to have a relationship of primitive sensation, of shallowness; to have a relationship on only the emotional level is to have a relationship overly focused on psychological issues; to have a relationship on only the spiritual level is to ignore that you are a feeling, breathing being.

But to have a relationship on all three levels is to acknowledge the beauty and complexity of being human. It is to be open—and to be filled by the incomparable possibilities that occur at the point of confluence of the physical, emotional, and spiritual dimensions.

At which level are you shortchanging your relationship? How can you expand it to encompass all three dimensions?

Beyond Dependence

*I*n our legitimate concern with unhealthy overinvolvement and, in particular, with dependence in our relationships, we can easily overlook the fact that relationships, in their very texture and nature, have as one of their highest potentials the possibility of healing us emotionally.

Of course if we don't carry a conscious ongoing concern for our own wholeness we can get sidetracked, detained, or even derailed in the process of somebody else's healing. But when we can see another person's tragedy as part of our own tragedy, and another person's healing as part of our own; we enter into the life-changing consequences of the healing power of love.

Are you overly involved with the person you love? Or is the love with which you are transforming his life also transforming your life for the better?

Amuse Yourself

*T*o be interesting, be interested. You are only as exciting as your own excitement, and one of the things you are obliged to offer to the person you love is the boon of your own involvement with life.

In a relationship we share not only what the person we love can give to us, but also who we are in ourselves. The books, music, fascinating hobbies (skydiving, cliff jumping, collecting wild snakes), or personal art forms (painting, ballet, photography, carpentry) that you pursue by yourself will also, through proximity, enhance the life of your beloved.

To be amusing, therefore, amuse yourself. What personally satisfying pursuit or amusement can you add to your current repertoire? And how will it spice up the stew of your relationship?

Rainbow of Needs

We all have an array of needs that crosses a wide spectrum. They can run all the way from needing new underwear, to needing your sweetheart to stop working so hard, to needing—right this minute—a touching conversation.

Our needs are like the flying buttresses that hold up the cathedral of our lives. Knowing them gives our lives structure; creating the circumstances that fulfill them gives our lives meaning.

So start right now to get acquainted with your needs. What do you need right this minute? What do you need in the next five years? What do you need for the rest of your life? Attend to your needs so that your life, when you leave it, will be a full circle of joy and not a broken circle of regrets.

Regaining Your Balance

$\mathcal{R}$ecovery means gaining back, returning again to the place or state of being you occupied before you got pneumonia, before you became an alcoholic, before you lost all your money in the stock market.

To forgive someone is a kind of emotional recovery, a going back to the state that existed before the wounding thing occurred, a deliverance from the constriction that prevails because you haven't been able to start over.

To regain your emotional balance today, try forgiving the person who hurt you—even if you don't want to, even if it seems impossible, even if what he or she did was unforgivable. Even if that person was yourself.

Give Yourself Distance

*W*hen you're ending a relationship (whether it's a friendship or a love affair), there's always the temptation to stay in touch with the person you're trying to leave. That's because we all need postscript experiences—little encounters that show us why we are leaving—that allow us to gradually tie up our unresolved emotional loose ends.

But keeping your distance is also a wonderful healer. If you've just ended a relationship and you're tempted to keep running back only to get rejected again, try to resist the temptation. As much as you can, keep your distance. In doing so you will discover some long-forgotten pieces of yourself—the attributes, possibilities, and surprising sense of excitement with which you can begin again.

Containing Joy

*L*oving yourself is imagining life as containing joy: joy in experience, joy in relationship, joy in the contents of your own being, joy in the delight that others feel in knowing and loving you.

What is the joy you feel in experience?

What is the joy you feel in your closest relationship?

What is the joy you feel with yourself?

What is the joy that others feel in knowing and loving you?

Unexpectedly Beautiful

When it comes to love (and a lot of other things too) we want what we want, when we want it, and in exactly the way that we want it. Being fanatically focused on the hows and whens of things keeps our attention on the abstract, and in the process we often miss out on the persons or things that come close to our dream because they weren't exactly what we had in mind.

Life isn't perfect. Our plans are never precisely fulfilled, but we are often and overwhelmingly surprised. Don't be fixated on your whims. Give up on your longing for things to be exactly the way that you want them to be in order to receive them exactly as they are.

Rite of Passage

*R*elationships have phases. This is no less true of friendships than of a lifetime romance. The transitions from one phase to another can be difficult, even heartbreaking at times, but they are also a rite of passage to growth and transformation.

These phases can't necessarily be orchestrated by the individuals involved. Rather, the relationship itself is following an organic unfolding that is a mystical synergistic response to and by the people in it. You will know that the passage has been completed when the troubling feelings have receded and unexpected new chapters of life have started to open.

What phase is your relationship in right now? The blush of new romance? The summer of depth and passion? The season of doubt and despair? Whatever it is, what can it teach you, in this moment, about yourself and the person you love?

The Healing Power of Love

*T*he reason there is so much substance abuse in this country is that, inside, people have so little substance. That's because they haven't received enough love. They have never been shown who they are at their depth, what their strengths are, what are the teachings of all their sorrows. Instead they've been told that what's outside—money, material things, distractions of whatever kind—is what matters the most.

We are a nation of addicts because we are a civilization of spiritual impoverishment. We can create organizations around our various addictive processes, but so far we have been unable to heal the spiritual deprivations that cause them in the first place.

Addiction is the search for transcendent experience. Its process is anguish and its healing is love. Today reach inside—for the depth of your wound, for the depth of your need—and reach out for the love that can heal it.

Breaking the Barriers

We all need to receive more: more love, attention, response, conversation, compliments, enjoyable time, empathy, recognition. But many of us are unable to receive the things that we most need. We're scared to know what we need (that would be facing a deficit, after all); and we're even more afraid of expressing it.

But learning what you need is the beginning of receiving. If it's still too difficult to identify what you need (sometimes we're as oblivious to our needs as the famished blind man is to the banquet table) start by identifying what you would like to receive.

What do you wish someone would give you? Words? Flowers? A wonderful lovemaking session? Some time to yourself? Starting now, try to tell yourself what you want. Because if you really, really want it, sooner or later, you will receive it.

Far Greater Than Death

*L*ife will not solve our sorrows, nor will it heal all our wounds. But the love we allow ourselves to feel, to receive, and to give, will be the thing that, after the party is over, after the final song has been sung, we will most remember, we will have been most changed by.

Nothing, not even the death of those we have loved, can separate us from the love we shared with them. For love is stronger far than death, and in the end the greatest gifts of love will be received again and again. Far more than we can imagine, we have been changed by those who have loved us, altered in every dimension, so that, at the center of our souls, they now inhabit us and we inhabit them.

The Hallmark of Fidelity

*F*or most of us, the sexual bond and the truth or lies we tell about it is what distinguishes a true love from all the others. Because our bodies carry our primal feelings, most of us need to be chosen exclusively in order to form the deep and abiding bond of nurturance and joyful sensation that makes us feel passionately connected to another human being.

For this reason sexual fidelity is the hallmark of most deeply bonded relationships. And when it is violated, broken through lies or dishonest behavior, a relationship that could once be held as a beautiful crystal vase becomes a vase that is marred forever by an irreparable crack.

We Who Serve

We who serve others—parents, teachers, healers, friends, human beings committed to the preservation and transformation of the planet—we, who hold so many in our arms and hearts and minds, need to be sure to experience interludes of refreshment. To be able to give lovingly of ourselves, we need the impact of new landscapes, nourishment for our bodies, and adventures for our souls.

Loving yourself is recognizing that your own life and energies are a chalice that can be emptied, and that, in order to continue serving you must replenish your own cup time and time again.

What can you do for yourself, what special experience, gift, or diversion can you give to yourself today so that tomorrow, refreshed and renewed, you will be able to serve once again?

Honor the Court Jester

*I*n each of us there is a hidden court jester, the fanciful spirit that always beholds the humor in life, who will, in the midst of any knotty problem or sad tragedy, distract us from our troubles by turning somersaults.

Staying in touch with this whimsical part of yourself, honoring and developing it, will fill your life with a lightness of spirit that keeps every worry at bay. But court jesters are shy: they won't stick around if they're not applauded. So if you want yours to continue performing, be sure to laugh when he juggles you out of your tears, and throw metaphoric confetti each time he whimsies your troubles away.

APRIL 9

Loving One Step Removed

*L*oving one step removed and giving thanks for those who love the ones you love is a wonderful way of expanding your circle of love.

For example, give thanks for the people who loved your wife before you met her: her mother, her first considerate sweetheart, the uncle who stepped in to take the place of her father; be grateful to your girlfriend's sister, the one who helped her become such a sensitive listener; cherish your husband's best friend; be glad that he filled the place of the brother your husband never had. Be solicitous on behalf of the friends of your friends.

These gestures of once-removed compassion create ever-expanding circles of love. They stretch out beyond the familiar landscapes of our lives to create acres of bondedness. They enlarge the sacred circle of our own community and connect us to all the other circles of love that are being continually drawn around us.

A Sense of Safety

*I*n order to be able to risk loving we need to be safe. We need to feel safe inside ourselves—with our feelings and our histories, with what we hope and imagine for our futures—and we need to feel safe outside ourselves—in the world, in our work, and with the people who profess to love us.

Safety, whether internal or external, is not intrinsic to situations or to our inner selves. Rather, it is a state that can be developed through the use of our own emotional powers of discretion. We become safe by being sensitive and using judgment.

To develop your own capacity for discerning whether or not you are safe in various situations, start asking yourself what you are sensing, feeling, and needing in a given situation; and then respond with a true answer. The more you do this, the more clarity you will get and the more your world will become the place of safety you need in order to thrive and flourish.

Expanding Your Repertoire

Most of us have three channels through which we experience love. We like to hear the words that speak of love, see the person who excites us to love, and experience the feelings that allow us to know, deep in our hearts, that we are, indeed, being loved.

Therefore, to be more loving and to feel more loved, be willing to expand the repertoire of your expressions of love. The person you love may need to feel your touch as well as hear your words, look into your eyes as well as hold your hand.

Today, take a minute to contemplate the various ways in which you ordinarily express your love. Then try to expand your repertoire. If you tend to talk, try touching more, if you tend to watch, try listening. The more ways you find to deliver your love, the greater and more profound will be your own experience of love.

APRIL 12

Pray for Love

*I*f you are feeling a great emptiness or lack of love in your life, remember that love is something you can ask for. Still your heart and your mind, open your soul, and ask for the love that you need—the love that can touch you and heal you—to be beautifully delivered into your life.

It may not come in the form you expect nor at exactly the time that you wish. But make no mistake, if you ask for love, unexpectedly, unequivocally, magically, and certainly, it will arrive.

APRIL 13

Do It Now

We don't have forever—to fall in love, to change our habits, to solve our problems, to figure out what we want to do with our lives. In just the same manner, we don't have an unlimited amount of time to say, do, feel, offer, deliver, share or enjoy all the things we can imagine saying, doing, feeling, sharing, or offering to the person we love.

So love the person you love right now—in the time you've been given to love her, in the ways you've been given to love him. Whatever you have in mind to do, whatever you've always imagined doing, do it now.

Because time vanishes. Things change. Stories end.

Life Itself

*H*ow easily we can forget how precious life is! So long as we can remember, we've just been here, being alive. Unlike other things for which we have a comparison—black to white, day to night, good to bad—we're so utterly immersed in life that usually we can see it only in the context of itself. We don't see life as compared to anything, to not-being-alive, for example, to never having been born. Life just is.

But life itself is a gift. It's a compliment just being born: to feel, breathe, think, play, dance, sing, work, and make love, for this particular lifetime.

Today give thanks for life. For life itself! For simply being born!

Letting Go

*N*o matter how hard you may try to end a relationship, it isn't over until it's over on every level for each person who was once a part of it. So long as either of you is still attached, the relationship remains—if only as a fantasy. So long as you are attached, by sorrow, anger, or disappointment, to the relationship of the past, you escape the joy of the relationships of the future.

Do you have any loose ends with someone that still need tying up? Are you still grieving for the husband who left you for another woman? Angry at the wife who abandoned you and your young children?

Whatever unresolved feelings you harbor, they are affecting your present capacity to love. Do yourself a favor and work them through, if need be with professional help. Because only when you have truly let go will you be able to take hold of something new.

Cradle for Our Souls

*T*here is no greater gift you can give to another human being than your response: to his tears, to his words, to his touch; to her hopes, to her dreams, to her prayers.

Response is joining; response is heartfelt participation. Response, of whatever kind—with your words, with your tears, with your heart, with your arms—is a way of standing inside the pain and the joy and the hope and the fear and the imagined isolation of another person's experience.

"I'm so sorry to hear that"; "That sounds awful"; "How wonderful; I'm so happy for you"; "You must be scared"; "I bet you're excited"; "I can't imagine how that must feel."

Respond. Respond with your heart. Respond as much as you can. Respond no matter how inadequate you feel. Response is the cradle in which, very gently, we rock one another's vulnerable souls.

No One But You

*I*n becoming ourselves, we often emulate others. We try to speak, think, dress, behave, or conduct our lives the way they do. We use their example, follow in their footsteps. In reaching for ourselves we model ourselves after them.

This process of copying is a good one—so long as we're sure that we're incorporating only those attributes and habits that really suit us. But sometimes we get lost in the process, admiring others so much that we completely lose track of ourselves.

If you've gotten lost in the maze of hero worship or guru groupiedom, remember that you, yourself, are the model, the hero, the best example of you. Be yourself—nobody else will ever do a better job of being you.

Transmuting Your Fears

*I*n addition to bringing us joy, relationships embody our specific fears: the man you love now comes home late every night, just like your father; the woman you love screams and raves when she's scared and upset, just like your mother. Indeed our present relationships embody all the fears and disappointments of our past. That's because in the present we need to revisit them and face them in order to see that we have survived them, that we are bigger than they are.

These upsetting reenactments invite us to reenter the forest of our old fears, to confront the mysterious monsters of the dark, and, having raged and grieved them, to come out into the sweeter, safer meadows of emotional enlightenment. Through the magical transmutation that can occur in any fully grown relationship, we can actually be healed.

What fears is your relationship inviting you to heal? Are you willing to confront them?

The Loss of Your Father

*N*o matter when your father dies, his death is a very moving experience, like the sound of a mighty tree that falls in the forest. Fathers are meant to protect us, to be the great existential umbrella, the giant wings of protection under which, in safety, in all weather, we can progress.

If your father loved you and gave you a comforting roof to cover your soul, you will feel exposed and vulnerable because of his absence, as if, unprotected because he is gone, you must face all the harshness of life now, raw and alone. And if he did not love you or loved you badly, you will feel the great gaping wound of never having been loved by him.

Whatever his mark on your life, his departure will leave you empty and changed, but in the void of his passing lies a surprising invitation: to discover in yourself your own capacity for fathering.

Nourishment for the Spirit

Words are food. They feed the spirits of the despairing and downhearted. They create happiness. They generate love. They alter the nature of reality.

Therefore, be generous with your words. Tell the people you love, and even the people who are strangers within your gates, the wonderful things you feel about them, because when it comes to nourishing words, the world is full of souls that are starving.

Love As It Is

So often we want to hold on to love because we think that's the way we can keep it. We want it so badly we squeeze it to death or we're so afraid it will leave that we chase it away. But the trick is to not try so hard.

Love wants us as much as we want it, but love wants us on its own terms, when it feels like coming, in the moseying time that it feels like arriving, with the plans that it has in mind.

So let go. Let go of your hopes, your dreams, and your fears, your beliefs about the way you think love ought to have been or should now be. Let go of love as you want it so that, finally, you can take hold of love as it is.

Face to Face

*M*aking love is a form of worship for your incarnation. It is a way of acknowledging with and through the presence of another person that we have come here in a form that longs to physically engage with one another. In making love we are attracted, we are drawn to, we are fulfilled. We are overjoyed by one another, time and time again.

Making love is pleasure and passion and compassion, affection, attention, and consolation. But it is more. It is coming face-to-face with the reality of being human, a spirit cocooned by physical being. Through making love we sing a thanksgiving simply for being alive, for possessing a body, and for the fact that in life, we do not entirely travel alone.

Healing Yourself

*H*ealing yourself, embarking on a path to self-illumination, whatever the discipline by which you accomplish it—prayer, meditation, yoga, the practice of love, inner emotional work, dancing, body building, psychotherapy—is the highest gift of love that you can ever give yourself.

Make a commitment to your own becoming by making a commitment to your own healing. Coming into the presence of your purest essence will deliver you to the greatest sense of joy that you can ever feel, the union of the God in you with the God in everyone else.

A Few Little Steps

Sustaining love is difficult. We want to enhance the bonds between us but often we don't know how. One of the reasons is that we don't know enough about ourselves to be able to identify exactly what we need or want.

Training yourself to know what you need, what you want, as simple as that may seem, is sometimes actually very difficult. But start today with a few little steps.

What would you like to receive from the person you love? Today? Before the year is out? What would you like to give to the person you love? Would he or she like to receive it? Are you willing to ask in order to find out?

What's a need of yours, completely apart from the person you love, that you hope will be fulfilled? If you've been able to ask all these things, you've made a really good start. Now, if you can tomorrow, carry on.

Love, the Essential

We all need the blessing of love. Whether or not we are gifted with a passionate soul mate for life, we all need to be loved by someone or something: pets, mothers and fathers, brothers and sisters, strangers, sweethearts, aunts and uncles, grandmothers, housekeepers, nannies, puppies, kittens, or cats. (My friend Kerry says he's okay because Crash, his goldfish, loves him.)

Love comes in many forms, and whatever its manifestations, we need to receive it, to swim in its blessing, to take it in. Love is the life force. Without love we die.

Where is the love in your life?

The Power of Truth

When you find yourself unable to tell the truth to the person you love, it is because somehow, together or separately, you have allowed untruth to enter into your lives.

Untruth consists of not telling and not risking as well as little white or big black lies. When untruth enters it stakes a claim on the integrity of your relationship and ever so gradually moves it in the direction of inauthenticity and separation.

If you want to be bonded and loved, seek the truth, receive the truth, and tell the truth; for truth is at the center of love, indeed it is love's very core.

Love Alters Time

*I*n life and in work we have hours, minutes, plans, and obligations. But love stops the clock. Love is time out of time. In it we measure things not in terms of what we have done, must do, or how soon or late we will do them, but in terms of bliss—of being suspended in a state where time and obligations are irrelevant.

This is one of love's greatest gifts: that it connects us with the endless eternal; it acquaints us with the beauty of timelessness.

How can you let the love that you feel, that is given to you by the people who love you, remove you for even the tiniest moment from the burdensome pressures of time?

Self-Honoring

*L*oving yourself means honoring your limitations as well as celebrating your strengths, forgiving yourself your faults as well as admiring yourself for your virtues.

Loving yourself is receiving yourself just as you are today with all your shortcomings, failings, and wounds. Today. Right now.

Love Is Worship

*L*oving another human being is worshiping God in the human form, being moved to awe that in each of us there exists not only a psychology and personality, not only habits and histories, preferences and predilections, but also the mysterious spirit that abides in each of us, the godlike essence that, through incarnation, has assumed the human dimension.

Therefore, when we love we not only celebrate another human being, we worship the god in him or her. Whomever you love, whatever the configuration of your relationship, reach for the perception that honors, acknowledges, and celebrates the presence of the divine in this cherished person.

APRIL 30

A Worthy Enterprise

*K*nowing yourself is the only worthy personal enterprise. If you don't know yourself you will live your whole life as though your were somebody else, without really attaining the things that warm your heart or fill your soul, without having the love that speaks to your needs, without accomplishing the things that are an honest reflection of your talents.

Knowing yourself is the rock on which to build the house of your life. It starts with asking the simplest question: What do I want or what do I feel right this minute? It then progresses through all the questions and reflections that in time will reveal to you the intricate refinements of your being.

So know yourself. You are the only person who can be yourself. You are the only person who can consciously and exquisitely discover who you are, the only person who can live your very special life.

The Atmosphere of Intimacy

We all seek intimacy, vaguely sensing that it is something wonderful, something that could bring us a world of happiness if only we could attain it. But intimacy is not a state to arrive at and just hang out in; it is an emotional atmosphere that you must constantly and consciously create together.

Intimacy is created with words that express the emotional closeness you feel and the closeness you desire, with the gentle gestures and touches that bring you into delicate proximity with the person you love, with the openness of heart that will allow you to give and receive.

Intimacy is a precious treasure and, like many other treasures, hidden or buried, it can only be found with conscious passionate intention.

Creating an Adventure

*M*ost people don't know how to create a union that is an adventure. Instead they experience their relationship as a container, a hatbox for an old romance.

Containment is the antithesis of adventure; and a relationship can be an adventure only when both people are genuinely crazy about each other and nobody's asking anybody to stop being himself or herself. It's important to remember that excitement lies in being open to the unexpected—not only to where your relationship will take you, but also to what each of you will become as a result.

So, if you want a relationship that is truly an adventure, be open to discovering the person you love as he endlessly, expressively, unfolds himself; don't spend your life remembering how it used to be or trying to get her to be the way she once was.

Both Male and Female

*I*n each of us there are both male and female components. We do certain things from the emotive, receptive, and sensitive side of ourselves that we often think of as being feminine, and do other things from an assertive, logical, problem-solving, typically male perspective.

Being in touch with yourself means that you acknowledge, honor, and celebrate not only the traits that are a reflection of your biological gender, but also the attributes that are traditionally a reflection of the opposite sex.

Today, watch with interest and excitement as you move back and forth between the male and female aspects of your personality.

Food for the Soul

*P*reparing a meal, taking your sweetheart out to dinner, passing your darling a morsel from your plate, spooning a dainty into your beloved's mouth—all these are sweet ways of nurturing one another.

For each of us food is the source of sustenance, the basis of life. When we offer this gift to the person we love we are not only nourishing each other's bodies; we are feeding one another's spirits.

Receive—and give—the food of your life as the powerful gift it is.

Conferring Meaning

We can view everything we do or fail to do, everything that happens to us and becomes of us, as either having meaning or as a meaningless event that occurs in a universe that functions in random meaninglessness.

Seeking to see the purpose and the lesson, exploring the message, believing that what you have done and will do, what befalls you and what you yourself create or inflict, is purposeful—that is the process of conferring meaning.

Viewing life, the world, and all your actions as meaningful is a way of acknowledging that at its center, at the core of its intention and in all the manifestations of its expression, the universe is bound together and sustained by overwhelming love.

Some Wounds Are Forever

*A*s resilient as they are, our children won't be able to get over all the hurts that, consciously or unconsciously, we inflict upon them. Some little ouches will heal because as parents we're sensitive and discover them and sooner or later apply the appropriate bandages. Others will be healed by friends and strangers who seem to appear out of nowhere to make up for the hurts we have caused.

But not all the nicks and scratches of childhood will be redressed. As parents we can cause irreparable damage, and as conscientious parents we need to remember that certain emotional and spiritual violations—heartless criticism, bitter judgment, broken promises, and endlessly repeated betrayals—can cause a door in your relationship not just to be slammed in your face, but, without your even noticing, to be locked forever.

When You Feel Unloving

Without our intending it, we can often stumble into being critical, mean spirited, and unloving. The circumstances of our own lives gang up on us and wear us out. We feel the ancient despair of certain life disappointments. Someone has judged us and in our own heart there is no longer room for kindness, no way to welcome the spirit of another human being.

When you find yourself lost in the pit of unlovingness—blowing up, being sarcastic, slamming the door—you need to recognize that these are signs that you have also stopped loving yourself. You have stopped seeing yourself with the compassion, which, if only you could reconnect with it, you could also offer to others.

Therefore make it your personal obligation today, and treat it as a moral responsibility always, to give some very gentle attention to yourself. For it is indelibly true that we can only love our neighbors when we have first been able to truly love ourselves.

Various and Abundant

*F*riendships are as various as flowers in the garden. Some, with almost no provocation, burst into bloom, flower briefly, then wilt and die down. Others, persnickety, need delicate tending to gradually blossom, starting with pale colors that slowly deepen with time. Still others bloom just once in a season, and after blooming, lie dormant until the sunshine of springtime can rouse them again. Yet others need constant pruning.

With friendships as with flowers variety is the hallmark of pleasure. It is the variousness and abundance of our friendships that make them a garden from which we can fill our hearts and feast our senses throughout our lives.

Psychological Consciousness

$\mathcal{P}$art of loving yourself is developing psychological consciousness, that is, being aware that you are a feeling
being who is endlessly affected by your emotions and your
history. This means seeing life not just in terms of what happens—it rained, my father died when I was seven, Johnny
broke his arm—but in terms of how you feel: rain makes me
sad; I've always felt ashamed because I didn't have a father;
I'm scared because Johnny got hurt so badly.

Psychological consciousness grants that there is more to
life than meets the eye, that the things that occur not only
passingly affect us, but also deeply shape who we are.

If you're not in touch with your psychological consciousness, take time to get acquainted with it now by starting to
pay attention to what you think, dream, and feel; by reading
about it; and, above all, by beginning to acknowledge that it
is always there.

Have Some Fun

We all have enough work in our lives—emotional work, housework, the work we do at our jobs, and the chores we do to keep our lives running smoothly. But rarely do we have enough play—distraction, diversion, amusement, pleasure, and just plain fun.

Having fun, figuring out what fun is for you, and finding the time to do it is sometimes one of the hardest jobs of a really good relationship. But it is vital to identify what you enjoy doing and then to do it. Play is the way you come home to each other. Play is what gives life its zest.

Take a walk. Play golf. Spend an afternoon in bed. Go hiking, go camping, go to the fair. Have some fun.

Love Takes Time

*F*ormulating love in such a way that we can express and enjoy it in a relationship takes time—the time it takes to know ourselves, the time it takes to communicate with another human being, the time it takes to become familiar with and sensitive to the patterns of another person's emotions and behavior.

Love doesn't just happen, and it certainly doesn't sustain itself without delicate intricate effort. The words, gestures, requirements, unfoldings, and responsibilities of love take more time than we can ever imagine and bring rewards much greater than we can ever dream.

You can be a good apprentice, a fine journeyman of love. But only if you give yourself time.

Don't Pass It On

Remember when you were in school and the kid behind you would hand you a crumpled note with a stupid joke on it and tell you to pass it on? You were supposed to be disgusted and then pass it on so somebody else could be disgusted too.

When we've been picked on by life, we often "pass it on" by picking on those around us. Little breaches of graciousness at times are unavoidable, but we need to remember that nothing that has been done to us can legitimately be passed on.

You can't blow up at your wife because your boss blew up at you. You can't spank your children because the plumber didn't come. We're all responsible to resolve, within the parameters of ourselves, whatever assaults have befallen us. We can ask for help, for consolation. But it is never right to simply "pass it on."

Of Moral Courage

When we have wounded or offended someone, we have a great many feelings. Among them are shame, embarrassment, self-loathing, and, as often as not, the desire, as one friend said to me, to simply "pretend that none of it happened."

To be at peace with ourselves and those we love when we violate another person's spirit, we need to bring it to resolution. Shame, self-loathing, and forgetting won't solve the problem; they only entrench bad feelings. Only forgiveness renews.

That's why, no matter what you have done, no matter how small or despicable your word or deed, you must have the courage to ask for forgiveness. Forgiveness does more than merely erase the terrible thing; it is an act of moral courage, a process of self re-creation.

What little or big thing do you need to be forgiven for? Do you have the courage to ask for forgiveness?

You're OK, I'm Terrible

A lot of us fall into the fantasy that everybody else's life is wonderful while ours is a clotted web of nightmares, heartaches, disappointments, and deviations from the norm. When we get into this state of mind, it's all too easy to stop caring on any level for other human beings.

When you find yourself slumped in this useless inhuman position, remember that every person suffers. Everyone has sufferings, should you bother to inquire about them, that would quietly blow your mind. Be aware of this, and if you have the courage, go one step further. The next time you're feeling overwhelmed, ask the first "normal" person you run into what's the most difficult thing that, at the moment, he or she is going through.

Then listen, watch your heart expand with compassion, and when you've rediscovered that you're not alone, dust off your membership card to the human condition.

Trusting Your Intuition

*I*ntuition, those vague little mental gnawings that make you think long before something happens that something wonderful or awful is about to occur, is a gift that all of us have to one degree or another. Our intuition is precious, something we need to learn to rely on. When we trust our intuition, we validate this very special part of our perceptual apparatus.

Trusting our intuition is an honoring of our spiritual dimension, for intuition operates outside the range of our normal field of perceptions and represents the mystical in us. When we trust it, we open ourselves to greater levels of understanding and belonging. When we ignore or ridicule it, we limit the scope of our being. The more you use it, the more refined it will become. Trust your intuition and watch you life undergo a mystical expansion.

Love Will Free You

*L*ove makes demands on us, especially when we express it in the form of an intimate relationship. But love itself is the embodiment of freedom, and whenever we experience real love, we know to the soles of our souls that we are free to be all that we dream, desire, imagine, and are. What do you need to do so that your relationship can grant a greater experience of freedom? To your beloved? For yourself?

Kissy Face

When we've matured to the point of having the luxury of making love, we can often forget and forgo the pleasures of simple affection—hugging and kissing, holding hands, hanging on one another's neck, cuddling up when we sleep, sitting on your darling's lap, running your fingers through your sweetheart's hair.

If sex is love's champagne, then affection is its hot cocoa. By indulging in the pure deliciousness of affection, we warm our bodies and satisfy our hearts.

Not Caring

W hen we're hurt, sometimes we try to tell ourselves we don't care: about the person who snubbed us, about the prize we didn't win, about the mean things that were said or done, the cruel words that were mindlessly spoken.

Not caring is a way of gradually not living, for in trying to not care, we imperceptibly cut off our feelings so that we also don't feel curious, don't feel happy, don't feel sad, don't feel angry, don't feel loving or loved.

The way through a hurt is to hold it close and to feel it, to shed the tears that will cleanse it and wash it away. Not caring leads to really not caring, in time to not living at all. So care! Feel, cry, and heal. So you can care once again. So you can live. So you can love.

Someone to Be at Your Side

Our existential aloneness, the fact that we are born and will eventually die alone, causes deep within us a longing for company, for someone to be at our side as we struggle through life's complex vicissitudes. Although we are all responsible for ourselves, although in some sense we all travel alone, our path is made sweet with company.

If you are fortunate and have been given a partner, acknowledge that you are lucky; be grateful. For the mere presence of someone to be at your side—familiar though she may have become, irritating as he sometimes may be—is not a given but, truly, one of life's miracles. And if you still seek someone to be at your side remember to consciously ask for it, for if you truly desire it, in time, it will surely be given.

Holding On and Letting Go

We all have things in our lives that we want to let go of and other things we wish to take hold of. There are experiences, people, possessions, habits, and points of view that we want to inhabit our lives more deeply, and others that seem to take up too much room.

Sometime during this day take a few minutes to contemplate, or better yet to write down, a list of all the things in your life that you'd like to let go of: habits, memories, attitudes, possessions, opinions, people. Do this quickly and spontaneously, and when you have finished, on the same piece of paper make a list of the things in your life that greatly nourish your spirit—the things, people, experiences, viewpoints, and ways of being you want to take hold of or hold more closely to yourself.

No Time Is Wasted

*I*n a relationship, there is no such thing as wasted time. The woman who wants to get married and insists that she is "wasting time" because her partner won't propose to her, and the disgruntled ex-husband who says he "wasted twenty years" with the woman he just divorced are both trapped in a very limited—and limiting—view of the meaning of relationships.

Every relationship has value; every experience we have in conjunction with another human being is just that—experience. We become who we are, we develop and refine ourselves, we are honed in preparation for the fulfillment of our highest destinies because of the time we "waste" with other human beings.

Every relationship teaches; every relationship, no matter its hardships, disappointments, or even its eventual dissolution, is of inestimable value.

Great Demands

A relationship isn't a panacea or a free-for-all. It isn't a place where you can just hang out and get yours. It is a very high undertaking, an energetic enterprise. After the moonlight comes the major transformations; after the roses comes the hard work.

Indeed, when you ask for a relationship you are asking to be extended in every dimension of your being, to transcend personal, social, cultural, and even gender boundaries, rules, and definitions. You are called upon to discover, through what love asks of you and gives to you, the things that are deepest in yourself, the things that will remain true in time beyond time.

Are you willing to open yourself to the great demands of love?

Getting a Hearing

*I*n any relationship everybody's trying to be heard. For most of us that's difficult, not just because it's hard to get people to listen, but because we ourselves often have a hard time finding the words and ways by which to make ourselves heard.

Today think hard about some very small or very large thing—just one—about which you'd like to be heard by the person you love. Write your message, if you need to, on a little scrap of paper. Then in a quiet moment, ask your darling if you can have an opportunity to say the thing you need to say and be heard, no matter what his or her inner response.

This is called getting a hearing, and once you have done it—especially if you feel listened to and responded to—you'll find that you have taken the first step toward always getting heard.

Keeping Current

*U*nfinished past relationships garble our capacity to receive the love that is coming to us now. They dull our mirrors, distort our reflection, confuse our perception, and make us think that new love is unavailable to us.

To be in the present with love, which means to be available to the love that is open to you now, you need to be willing to go through the cleansing, healing, grieving, and gratitude that will deliver your past to the past and your self to the present.

What is your unfinished business with your past relationships? Think about what buried anger and sorrow, what unacknowledged fears, what unexpressed thanks you need to express in order to bring yourself into the present with your love.

The Cup of Sorrows

*H*ow can we love those we love when they are going through a dark time—depression, discontent, the emotional fallout from losses and disappointments that are cruel or unbearably unfair?

Our tendency is to ignore them because we feel helpless, to wait out the difficult time, to hope that the trouble will pass or, if we make an attempt, to try to deny that the bad thing has happened. Instead of commiserating, we cheerily say it really isn't so bad or that something better will come along.

But all these are shallow measures. To be with others in their sufferings, we must be willing to join them, to drink from the cup of their sorrows knowing that, although we can't take the cup from their lips, its bitterness will be lessened because we have sipped from it with them.

Express Your Discontent

*T*here are three ways to handle people who offend you: Take note of their offense and keep quiet about it; blow up and bring negative attention to yourself; or openly and clearly tell them how you feel about what they have done.

Keeping your mouth shut can lead to acting out your resentment in some sideways fashion later (showing up late for the birthday party, "forgetting" to pay back the money you owe). Blowing up makes you look as though you're the one with the problem.

But being direct allows both of you to be honored. You honor yourself by revealing the limits of what you will accept, and you honor the other person by inviting him to become more conscious of the effects of his conduct.

Fear of Loneliness

One of our most common fears is loneliness. We fear those moments, days, and conditions in which we are without company or distraction, in which there is no other person to keep our attention away from ... ourselves.

The fear of loneliness is really the fear of facing ourselves, the fear that, should we be alone with ourselves, we may encounter great emptiness. The truth is that loneliness can be a deep and creative state. Where we fear we will find nothing, we can actually discover so much—the truth of our souls, our feelings, memories, and longings, our inner peace, our quiet connection with everyone and everything else.

So don't be afraid of loneliness. Allow yourself to visit it. Allow it to inhabit you, for through it you will surely gain a more profound experience of yourself.

The Map of Your Body

O ur bodies are the map of our lives and carry the messages of what we have been through. They reveal the price we have paid for all that we have learned: the aching back, the pins in the ankle, the reconstructed jaw. In this process our bodies will not remain endlessly new; they carry the scars of how our spirits have been tested, and in the end they will break down because our spirit's journey has been completed.

So treasure your body as the Rosetta stone it is, the blackboard on which has been written the story of your life. Cherish the scars, take note of the meaning of the changes and the marks. And rather than desperately trying to preserve your body as it was when you were young, receive its changes as the mirror of a life richly lived.

Good Things Are Real Too

*M*ost of us have experienced enough overwhelming heartaches and disappointments in life to, at one time or another, feel as though only the hard things are true. We all know a proponent of the "It's Always Something" school of thought, someone whose world view is that life is awful, all suffering and pain.

To believe that good things are real too, to affirm life even with its difficult lessons, to embrace its joys and celebrate its myriad little wonders and endless curiosities, to be astounded by its beauty—this is an act of faith. It is faith in life itself. And we allow ourselves to love life, to receive it as an act of love, a gift of grace, life then, and only then, can it become worthy of the faith that we have placed in it.

Praise Your Beloved

*D*on't be afraid to praise the person you love, to open your mouth and say all the beautiful things you feel in your heart:

"Your courage gives me hope."

"Your honesty gives me faith."

"Your gentleness gives me comfort."

"Your energy gives me energy."

"Thank you for coming into my life."

Praise, praise your beloved today!

Showing the Way

One of the tasks of being alive is to pass on the lessons you have learned to those who come after you. This is a natural function of parenting, of being involved grandmothers and grandfathers or nurturing teachers.

But we can also serve this function for any younger person who crosses our path. When we take someone under our wing—a co-worker, a fellow traveler, the friend of one of our children—and give them loving attention, direction, and example, we give them the benefits of our expertise in living and loving. In so doing we are showing the way, allowing the love that has shaped us to be passed on to them so that in ever-expanding circles, we influence the world.

Between You and Love

*B*etween you and the love you desire stand many barriers, some of your own making. This is true whether you are seeking a relationship or whether the full intensity of love has eluded you in the relationship you have.

To begin to break down the barriers, ask yourself the following questions: What in my circumstances is holding me back from experiencing the love I need? What habits, outdated commitments, irrelevant or unhealthy relationships are preventing me from having access to the love I want? (List and describe them.)

What attitudes about love do I need to change? (For example, the notion that love is what happens to other people.) What fears do I need to face? What memories do I need to heal?

And finally, what, exactly, are the words I need to say to focus my intention for love so perfectly that I will receive precisely the love that I need?

Seeing and Being Seen

*T*he person who loves you will not only see you but show you to yourself. This means that in love you will constantly be presented with reflections, reactions, images, affirmations, and confirmations of yourself. In time, these reflections will truly allow you to see who you are.

The "seeing" will come in many forms: words, touches of the eyes, gestures of the hands, gifts, surprises, memories, hopes, and dreams.

How do you want to be seen? Can you let the person who loves you begin to see you more deeply? And what can you say, do, give, ask, so the person you love will feel more truly seen by you?

Honoring Your Needs

*B*eing aware of your needs is a form of loving yourself. Many of us were taught to ignore our own needs, put others' needs ahead of our own, or treat our needs as though they were embarrassing or shameful and ought to be suppressed.

Some of what we need: sustenance, care and protection for our bodies, nurturing for our attributes, company on our journey, peace for our delicate spirits. To dishonor or ignore your own needs, whether basic or extraordinarily unique, is to treat yourself as if your existence is a joke, your personality unworthy of the beneficence of life.

So if you have shrouded your needs in the needs of others or if you simply haven't yet become acquainted with them, take time to make a list of some things you need right now. Then watch as your unconscious gradually allows you to fulfill them.

JUNE 4

Cherish the Moment

*T*he moment you are living through is exquisite in its uniqueness. It has never happened before. It will never happen again.

Whatever you are doing—writing a book, watching the sunset, kissing your sweetheart, watering the zinnias, making love—allow yourself to receive the experience deeply. For to be in the moment is to be fully alive, to recognize at the level of your very cells that life itself, the weather, the clouds, the talents you possess, the people you love are utterly unique and absolutely unrepeatable.

To live in the moment is to live. Live now!

With Yourself

When we think of relationships, we usually think of the relationship we have with someone else, a sister or brother, a parent, a lover, a friend. But there is a very unique relationship with a special person that most of us overlook: the relationship with oneself.

This relationship is formed through conscious focused attention on ourselves. In it we discover who we are, what we like and dislike, what moves and touches us, where our hurts are, what we hope for, the myriad of people and experiences that have shaped us, what we want out of life, and what we want from ourselves.

What we get from this relationship is depth and texture of experience. We get to know a person from the inside; we discover the intricate exquisite beauty of a single human being, the magic of ourselves.

Connected Forever

*Y*ou are deeply connected to anyone you have ever loved or whose love has changed your life—no matter whether the relationship changes or even comes to an end, no matter whether you are separated by time, distance, experience, or even death.

What becomes of you because you love and have been loved will last forever; the changes that occur in you are recorded in the very molecules of your being.

To whom are you connected forever?

Parents Need Children

We tend to assume that parenting—the selfless giving out of love, nurturing, advice, instruction, emotional and financial support—is a natural and utterly fulfilling state for anyone who is a parent. But this simply isn't the case.

Few of us have been so generously parented ourselves that we have the ability to be truly selfless in our giving. In fact, many of us arrive at the portal to parenthood so badly deprived of parenting that rather than being able to parent our children we want them to parent us.

Acknowledging your own need for love from your children will protect you from indulging in one of the worst abuses of children by parents: appropriating them as parents or spouses for yourself. Therefore don't be afraid to express how much you need your children to love you. That way their love can be a favor they take pleasure in giving, and your love will also, truly, be a gift to them.

The Poignancy of Change

Change always invites us into a soft little sadness. We are sad about losing what we must let go of and scared of what will arrive in its place.

Change is mystery past our control. Fear makes us see it as loss, but love allows us to see it as possibility—the birth of the new, which, aside from the presence of love, we would be too afraid to envision for ourselves.

Today, allow yourself to embrace the changes in your life. Savor the mystery; open to the surprise; remember that change is benefaction of love.

Separate and Together

O ne of the most difficult problems in any intimate union is how to have the relationship while still being able to retain a sense of yourself. Selves can get lost in relationships especially if they weren't very sturdy or fully formed in the first place.

To keep track of yourself in a relationship, you need to be continually aware of who you are, what you are feeling, and what your needs are. You can do this very simply by making a list every morning that answers the following questions: What am I feeling right now? What are my needs for this day?

In addition, remember that there are always three persons in any intimate relationship, "I," "You," and "Us." Make sure that at all times you are taking care of the "I" as well as the "You" and the "Us."

The Ballast of Friendship

*F*riendship is the boon of company, the sense of being joined on our journey. It is through the experience of feeling no longer alone that we come to believe that life will be full of surprises, that magical things will happen.

Friendship is what steadies us. Friendship gives us a footing. Friendship is comfortable. Friendship has seasons. Friendship is cozy. Friendship is easy. Friendship is forever.

In the Valley of the Shadow

*M*ost of us are so afraid of death that one of the most difficult tasks of love is being with someone who is dying. We feel embarrassed and strange. We bumble around, trying to ignore the blatant fact that, while we are staying, they are leaving this world.

If someone you love is dying don't be afraid to partake of the experience. Remember the times you have shared and happily talk about them; thank her for what she has taught you, the gifts you have received. Invite him to talk about his past, his joys and triumphs, his sorrows, fears, and regrets. Thank her for sharing a part of this lifetime with you.

You may feel strange, but remember that no matter how inadequate your attempts may be, they will be much better than no attempt at all. They will be a final wrapping of love around your relationship.

The Gift of Time

*F*or most of us, there's not enough time. Most of our time is spoken for by: work, by the endless demands of family, by the many inescapable obligations—bills, laundry, cleaning, looking after the cares of so-called "daily life." Unfortunately there is very little time left, after doing all we must do, for the precious things of life: for loving others, for discovering ourselves.

However, your time is your life, and at the top of the list of all the people who need to have some of your time, should be yourself. So today, as a way of loving yourself, take a few minutes to consider what kind of time you would like to give to yourself—to read, to walk, to meditate, to go for a run on the beach—and make a commitment, not just for today, but for everyday, to give yourself the gift of time.

Finding the Bridge

Some people are easy to get to know. They're attractive, outgoing, and talkative. They inquire about us, they reveal themselves. They have open spirits, and in their presence we have a nice experience of them and also of ourselves.

Other people are difficult, shy, or closed off by their pain. They may have great gifts to offer, wonderful insights or lessons from the crucible of their experience, but somehow they don't have "a bridge" to others, a way of presenting themselves. We don't know how to reach them; they don't know how to reach us.

With such people we need to carry the bridge: the compliment, "What a pretty blouse," or the question, "Where did you grow up?" that gradually opens them up. When we build the bridge we give love and open the bridge for more love—and other miracles—to start coming back to us.

Homespun and Holy

*C*onsideration means that as you conduct your life you think of, feel for, contemplate on behalf of, and carry concern about others—and not only yourself.

Consideration is a homespun, holy, wonderful attribute of love. It's homespun because it doesn't take genius. It's holy because it elevates the quality of what is happening. It's wonderful, because it makes things run more smoothly, makes everyone—including you—feel infinitely better.

Your Brothers and Sisters

*Y*our own brothers and sisters may not be the people whom you can love most easily. They may look like you because you have the same parents, and in a number of other ways you may share the same family traits. But on a deeper level you may feel as though you are a stranger in their midst.

The families of our birth encompass our childhoods and contain our biological siblings. But only many years later, in wonderful friends and amazing strangers, may we discover the brothers and sisters in spirit who comprise our truest family.

Forgive Yourself

*T*here are things you have done and will do that disappoint, hurt, or batter the trust of the people you love. You can't be perfect even if you try. (Of course you should try to be as good as you can be.) But when a thoughtless word, an inappropriate gesture, or an unintentionally devastating disclosure harms someone you love, you need to first of all forgive yourself.

Apologize of course, and ask the person for forgiveness, but also be willing to forgive yourself. It's hard to see our own flaws, to see our limitations mirrored in another's disappointment, to make a mistake and still love ourselves. But you deserve to be forgiven, to be given another—or a dozen other—chances to start over.

So after you've apologized, look at yourself with compassion, and forgive the you who, for whatever reason, was unable to enact the goodness that is really your highest essence.

Love Suffers

*A*long with being delicious, sweet, a happy miracle, and the answer to all your dreams, love suffers and endures. That is, love goes through things because the caring that love embodies is willing to go on the journey, even to the depths of difficulty and despair, with another human being.

This is not co-dependence or masochism; it is the creative, transforming sacrifice of love. For when love suffers, love of an even greater depth and strength is miraculously created.

Although you may be discouraged, even frightened, about the appropriateness of what, at times, you have gone through on behalf of those you love, allow yourself to honor what your sacrifices have accomplished. For suffering is also an important part of love.

Spiritual Richness

We are brokenhearted because our spirits are starving. We want and need the deep experience. As healthy human beings our appropriate response would be to cherish people and use things, but our culture presses us instead to use people and treasure things. This turnabout of our most instinctual inclinations grates on us at an unconscious level. We feel deprived of the healing magic we intuitively know could set our spirits free.

Spiritual richness, basking in the love that makes us feel intimately connected, is not a thing we can buy nor something that society encourages. It is won in the quiet of our own hearts, nurtured through steady discipline, and affirmed by the accumulating presence of real love.

To fill your spirit, know first that it longs to be fed. Then consciously seek those persons, experiences, and practices that will genuinely nourish it.

Open or Closed?

*C*ommunication that makes it safe for another human being to reveal himself, to open the inmost reaches of herself and make them visible to you, is open communication. It contains an invitation and is devoid of judgment: "How are you feeling?"; "What did that mean to you?"; "Why was it so difficult?"

Conversely, communication that contains criticism, judgement, or attack—"You shouldn't have done that anyway"; "You always were spoiled"; "That's the ugliest dress I've ever seen"—ensure that the other person will close up like a clam.

Open communication enhances intimacy while closed communication squelches it. So watch how you speak to the person you love. Make what you say sound like an invitation to a party, not like the handing down of a lifetime prison sentence.

Call to Power

*H*onoring your need for love will take you to the place where you can use your power. In discovering and nurturing the places in you that were abused or deprived, you will gradually receive what was missing and be made whole.

When you have grieved your losses and repossessed your gifts, you will become able to perceive yourself in an entirely new way, as whole, as capable. Gradually, you will have the freedom to discover and enact what is yours, precisely, in this life to do. And ultimately you will feel the joy of using the power that is uniquely yours.

What difficult things in your past are you still afraid to look at? How are they preventing you from coming into your power?

Intelligence Set Free

*I*ntuition is intelligence set free, the mind loping along outside the boundaries of conventional perception. Intuition is a function of love because it discovers not what we expect, but what we might never have imagined.

When we trust our intuition we trust ourselves. We imagine, believe, and expect that there is more to understand than our conscious mind by itself can get a grasp on. We "go for it." We invite the unexpected to happen.

So what's standing in the way of your trusting your intuition? What happens when you do? What's happened when you haven't? Acknowledge, respect, and enjoy your marvelous intuition.

More Affection

*A*ffection is the physical sweetness of life. With it we touch one another, literally on the surface and also at the depths.

We really do need affection. One of my friends says he "died in his skin" because he was never touched as a child. Affection—soft touches, warm hugs, and sweet kisses—is healing. It soothes our bodies, buoys up our spirits, and changes the way we feel about everything.

It isn't just our darlings or sweethearts who need affection: we do, too. And so do our friends, our children, our dogs and cats. So stop reading this and give somebody a dose of affection right this very minute!

Curbing Possessiveness

*I*f because of your own insecurities or fears of abandonment you find yourself feeling possessive, try to break through this by remembering that the very presence of someone to love in your life is something of a miracle. Instead of controlling or possessing—and as a consequence receiving only a portion of the love that you could—back off. Try to look at what you're afraid of and why you feel safe only when you possess or are possessed by somebody else.

Who left you? Who didn't love you enough? What are you afraid of losing (or gaining) if you lose control of the person you're trying so hard to possess?

What You're Afraid Of

*D*on't be afraid to be afraid. Being scared is a way of telling yourself you have limits, that inside you're still childlike, that you haven't been entirely hardened by practicing the toughening conventions of adulthood. So you're afraid, why shouldn't you be? Life is difficult, unfair, and scary; recognizing that fact is, paradoxically enough, a wise part of being a grown-up.

Noticing what you're afraid of also invites you to love yourself with a greater degree of refinement, to respect yourself for what you can't handle, as well as for all the ways in which you're big and brave and strong. Your fears invite you to ask to be loved not just when you've got it all under control, but even when you feel shaky, shattered, and small.

The Sacred Circle

*M*aking love doesn't exist in a category by itself. When you enter the sacred circle of sexual intimacy, you are inviting yourself to partake of a profound emotional relationship, a spiritual encounter.

To treat sex as anything less is to shortchange yourself and, unwittingly, to bring yourself into the presence of a nameless sorrow. So honor your sexuality as the mysterious and beautiful power it is, and it will give back to you more than you ever imagined.

Your Imperfect Parents

*O*nly when you have felt your anger at your parents will you be able to feel your compassion for them. Only when you allow yourself to see how they have wounded you will you be able to see the ways in which, as well as they could, they also loved you.

Feeling your anger will allow you to see them as multidimensional human beings with wonderful attributes as well as painful foibles. It will release you from the prison of being their victim and them from the cage of their role as your parents.

If you haven't already resolved your anger at your parents, allow yourself to begin the process today by at least identifying the content of your anger at each of them and by trusting that in time you will be able to move toward compassion.

Dashing Expectations

*L*ove creates expectations that wonderful things will happen, at a certain time and in a certain way. We have plans for what will become of us; we think our love story will turn out to be just the way we imagined.

But relationships have a tendency to dash our expectations. We are called upon to act, to change, to become, and not always in the ways that we wished. We find ourselves living not according to our dreams, but according to the demands of reality. This can make us feel angry, disappointed, and gypped.

If your dreams have turned to ashes because of the demands of your relationship, don't despair. Remember that in the process you have been cleansed by the fire of transformation, for in dreams we are always passive—life happens to us—but in reality we act, expand, and grow.

Whipped Cream

*C*ompliments are the whipped cream and maraschino cherries of life—unnecessary but especially delectable. We can all live without them, accomplish what we need to, and survive. But compliments lift our spirits, and give us a sense of our specialness and value, and added pleasure in being alive.

A compliment is a tiny little present, some rhinestones on the plain gray flannel suits of our lives. It may seem simple, but in offering a compliment, we offer love in one of its purest, most selfless forms—words for no other purpose than to make another person feel good.

The Devotion of Love

*F*or most of us love is the feeling we have in relationship with another human being, camaraderie, recognition, shared goals, the enjoyable passing of time.

But there is a form of love that goes beyond love as we commonly know it and this is love as devotion. Here love is not so much infused into our daily lives as it is itself the state of being that we offer as a gift.

When we practice love as devotion we are called to the most profound level of our being, invited to open our hearts and offer the singing of our spirits in honor of the divine that resides in every other human being.

In devotion we serve with our all, whatever the price, no matter how long it may take. We offer our love as the highest contribution we can make, and we offer it with our whole hearts.

Don't Be Closed-Hearted

*B*eing closed-hearted is being afraid to ask for the miracle you desire: that you will find your form of expression, that you will have company, that you will have health, that you will be delivered from your addiction, that you will have peace of heart, that your children will flourish, that you will be loved.

Ask for the miracle; open your heart!

The Emotional Web

*A*ll emotions are interconnected in an exquisite and beautifully woven web on the unconscious level. This is why, even when our emotions seem disparate, disconnected, and confusing on a conscious level, when we examine them more deeply we can see that they are intricately connected. It is also why our dreams, which may seem meaningless or ridiculous, once understood reveal to us the incredible beauty of the functioning of our consciousness.

While your dreams may seem a mystery to you, the more you give attention to what your unconscious is trying to reveal to you through them, the more you will respect and be genuinely awed by the beauty of your emotional life.

Make a commitment to remembering your dreams and begin to write them down, and you will find that you will remember them more easily and begin to comprehend their important meanings.

Love Is a Prayer

*L*ove is a prayer for: connection, communion, continuity; security, passion, compassion; magic and music; forgiveness; fun and frolic; a future; coming home.

When we ask for love we are asking for all these things. And when we are loved we have a sense of having been given them. Our prayer has been answered; our lives have been enriched.

A Deep Loss

*T*he death of one's mother is many things—the end of the bond with the person who originated us, the closing of a relationship that shaped and frustrated us, a hole in the fabric of our lives.

A mother's love is the staff of our lives; if we had it, we grieve its departure; if we were not gifted with enough of it, we grieve the forever-empty place.

If your mother has died, may your heart be filled again, anew, with the love you did receive from her; and in the absence created by her departure, may you claim the mothering spirit in yourself.

Passing the Transference Test

*T*ransference, imagining the person who loves you now will betray you the way you were betrayed in the past, is one of the greatest detours on the road to love.

Discovering how your beloved is both like and not like the person you fear him to be is a way of moving through transference and into a genuine emotional relationship.

Avoiding this is possible, but not easy. First you need a map of your past. You need to know exactly who hurt you and how. Then you need to be willing to step through your fear—that she will be just like your mother, sister, father. Finally, you need to invite the person you love to reveal herself as she is, to tell you her real hopes and fears. Discovering that he is not the person you remember from the past moves you through the blindness of transference and into the light of true intimacy.

Hard Traveling

*T*he road to love is paved with potholes. It's not a four-lane, high-speed, great-scenery freeway. Rather it's a little back road that moseys through beautiful countryside; you stop for a picnic now and then, are often late to your destination, and sometimes wonder if getting there was worth all the trouble.

Knowing this about your relationship will encourage you to be more patient when, against your hopes and wishes, the road doesn't simply—and without so much as a detour—unravel in front of you.

Being realistic generates tolerance of yourself, of your partner, of the process. Love is a beautiful journey, but the road can be bumpy and slow as well as fast and exhilarating.

Emotional Etiquette

*I*n spite of the blessing and comfort of a relationship, it isn't a free-for-all. The privilege of being related to another person doesn't mean, for example, that you can drop your social, emotional, or spiritual etiquette.

The manners of an emotional relationship are the etiquette of everywhere else, only more so. That means you should address the person you love by name, with terms of endearment. Say please and thank you; don't simply give orders or boss your partner around. Remember that special gestures of acknowledgement or praise can make all the difference, even for the simplest of things: "That was a beautiful dinner"; "You look so handsome tonight."

Treat the person you love like company.

JULY 7

Your Spiritual Equals

*J*ust because you're a parent doesn't mean you have a right to abuse your children. Parenthood isn't a license for condescension, pontificating, or self-righteous self-indulgence. Pulling rank on your kids because of your role—"Because I'm your mother (father), that's why"—isn't right. In fact, it's a travesty of the privilege of having children in the first place.

So honor your children by treating them as children when it comes to their physical and emotional needs. But remember that they're people too. Aside from what, because of your age and experience, you have to teach them, at the core they are your spiritual equals.

Befriending Your Loneliness

When you're afraid of your loneliness think of it as a strange, exotic animal, a wild creature with which you have yet to get acquainted. It's scary, this curious animal, because it's unfamiliar. You don't know how to treat it; you don't know how it will treat you.

But loneliness, accepted, can turn to aloneness, and aloneness, in time, to solitude. Solitude is a beautiful, quiet state, one in which, instead of fearing the strange mysterious animal, you can look into its eyes and come quietly face-to-face with the beauty in yourself.

JULY 9

Out of Balance

Self-centeredness is self-love out of balance, putting yourself first, second, third, fourth, fifteenth, and twenty-third in every situation. Self-centeredness is not true self love, a realistic appraisal of your value and an honest presentation of yourself. Rather, because you aren't entirely sure you exist, have value, or will have impact in any situation, you tediously display and overassert yourself.

Self-centeredness is difficult on others, but it's also hard on you. It doesn't allow you to have the kinds of emotional exchanges in which you both affect and are affected by those around you.

Try to notice the big or little ways you get carried away trying to be the center of attention. See if you can identify the fear that lies beneath it and step over or around it by inviting someone else to talk about him- or herself.

For Everyone

Whatever we're going through, whatever pains are inviting us to change, whatever love is breathing new life into us, revealing the presence of the divine at our center, we are receiving these transformations of growth and of healing not only for ourselves but for everyone, for the whole human race.

The changes that are alive in us, the love that is reshaping our hearts and restructuring our individual possibilities, are the blueprint of tremendous change for everyone.

Every feather on the bird's wing carries the beautiful bird a little bit closer to home. Every moment of love each one of us feels brings us all a little bit closer to the moment of our ultimate reunion.

Honoring Genius

Genius is spiritual intelligence, the mind operating outside the boundaries of formal education, known parameters, and perception as we commonly know it.

Genius, because of its extraordinariness, is often tragically mistaken for failure or limitation, is castigated, abused, or ignored. Therefore, the capacity to honor genius is a kind of genius in itself. Honoring genius is a highly developed function of love.

How can you honor the genius among you, the unsung genius in yourself?

The Healing Journey

*A*ny healing process, whether getting over pneumonia, recovering from an addiction, grieving a death, or mourning the end of an intimate relationship, is a complex journey with thousands of intricate steps.

At its outset we never know how long the journey will be, how many tears or how much blood will be spilled on our path. We begin it only because we know vaguely that we desire to be healed. The true depth of our need to be healed and the rewards of our healing are illuminations that we will receive only after, blindly but in good faith, we have taken the first few delicate steps of the journey.

What healing process are you in the midst of or have avoided undertaking, and how can you tiptoe toward it today?

Growing Up

Emotional maturity is one of the greatest achievements of psychological awareness. It is the antithesis of emotional immaturity, which expresses itself whenever it wants to, in whatever fashion it feels like, no matter what the consequences.

Hysteria, pouting, manipulation, whining, withdrawal, sarcasm, attack—all these are forms of emotional immaturity. They show that the person enacting them is still emotionally young, still not strong enough to act maturely.

When we are emotionally mature, on the other hand, we know that the world does not revolve around us, that solutions to problems, whether circumstantial or emotional, take time and will not necessarily come in exactly the form we imagined.

Emotional maturity has patience, knows when to hold its tongue, and when to offer a comforting word. Emotional maturity is a fine art. Develop yours.

Play Today!

*B*eing playful is the cotton candy of any meat-and-potatoes relationship. It's the devil may care, let's have a party, let's skip work and go to the beach, let's rent three videos and watch them all tonight state of mind that lifts a relationship from the tedious and banal to the extraordinary and effervescent.

We forget to play or we never learned how. We are worked so hard and so long by life as it is, and by our own ambitious demands, that most of us don't play nearly enough.

So why not take the opportunity of this beautiful day to entice your partner into a little playful mischief? Do something entirely spontaneous; let it take you where it may.

Stretching Your Heart

*I*t's relatively easy to love those who are close to you, your family and friends, the people who share your habits and values. But to love misfits and strangers, persons whose approach to life is in no way like yours—the bag lady at the drugstore counter, the strange old man who rides through town on a three-wheel bike all strung up with flags—that's much more difficult.

The person who doesn't fit in with our notions of who is worthy of love is just the person who, by not fitting into our patterns, insists that we expand not only our views but also our capacity to love.

Today see if you can stretch your heart and expand your love so that it touches not only those to whom you can give it easily but also those who need it so much.

Discovering Your Deservingness

*T*elling ourselves "I deserve" something rarely allows us to truly receive it, for at our core we all know we are imperfect beings and the "I deserve it" school of thought will rarely fool our sensitive psyches.

On the contrary, it is through gratitude, by saying thank you, that we discover our deservingness. For in saying thank you we experience ourselves as having received something, and in the receiving we are given a sense of our value.

Saying thank you is the beginning of discovering your own deservingness.

With Your Time

*L*ife is the gift of time, time on earth, time to be a body, time to have a personality, time to have the myriad lovely and difficult experiences we call life. Indeed, the way we spend our time creates the very quality of our lives.

Therefore, what we do with our time is very important. Whether we use it to do things that nurture our spirits or waste it mindlessly in time will make all the difference. For in the end we will see whether in life we have had "a good time" or whether, having wasted time, we wish we had had more of it.

So take care with your time, this precious beautiful gift, and treat it as the treasure it is. Today, take note of each hour that is given to you and choose, with your heart and your mind, exactly what you want to do with it.

The Challenge of Patience

*P*atience is waiting for reality to catch up with what we've already imagined.

Patience takes courage: it asks that we will be brave through the uncertainty of the unfolding. It takes faith: it asks that before the evidence comes in to prove our hunch, we will nevertheless keep believing that the beautiful thing can happen.

Patience is a virtue because it never comes easily; patience is a discipline that requires we stretch beyond our limits. Patience is holy, an exercise for our spirits. Patience is an act of love because unless we love ourselves we will never be able to undertake it.

JULY 19

Feeling Left Out

We can feel left out for a number of reasons. We feel left out because we are different. We feel left out because, unintentionally or with cruel intention, others hurt us. We feel left out because we are alone. We feel left out because we are insecure, have limitations, didn't get chosen, or are standing on the outside (of the family, the club, the meeting, the candy store) looking in.

Feeling left out is a consequence of feeling unloved. We feel left out when no one has loved us or when the thread of love that could draw us in is tattered or broken.

When we feel left out we want to break down, but we need instead to reach out and do a very difficult thing: Instead of waiting for someone to throw us a rope, we need to weave it ourselves and lasso love in.

Happily Wasted

*I*ntimate time is time in which you do nothing—nothing, that is, that you ordinarily do: wash dishes, make lists, take care of the car, read the newspaper.

Intimate time is private time, time for the "we" and the "us" of your relationship. It's do-nothing, no-obligation time, time when you mindlessly talk, lazily sit around on the couch, or happily and cozily make love.

Intimate time is time happily wasted, but it is also time of great value. For it is time that softens your heart, cements the bonds of your love, quietly forges the strength of even the best relationship.

Take intimate time.

The Sun of Love

*L*ove is the sun, the light that casts shadows of brightness in even the darkest of times. Love will hold you, console you and nourish your spirit; it will smooth your brow and wipe away your tears. Love is the infinite eternal parent, the mother who will never abandon you, the father who will never abuse you. Love will step in for the mother who never held you, the father who never encouraged you.

Love will heal your heart and satisfy your soul. Allow yourself to be nourished by its fabulous, stunning power. Allow all its beautiful brightness to fall into your face until, as love, you are reborn.

Finding Forgiveness

*H*ow can you ever forgive and find room again in your heart for the person who has failed you, the person you loved who betrayed you, the person who disappoints you over and over again in spite of the fact that you love him?

To forgive the person who has failed you is a spirit-enlarging process. It requires that you recognize that you too are imperfect, are capable, for no reason or any reason, of wounding another person just as much as you've been wounded.

Forgiveness is coming to see that you yourself partake of the imperfect humanness that for the moment is being embodied by the person who has failed you. To forgive is to see the other person's failure as a reflection of the general human imperfection and not as an intentionally cruel violation focused squarely on you. Forgiveness expands your perspective. If you are having difficulty forgiving, consider your own imperfections.

All of Our Being

*I*n this very psychological and physical-fitness-oriented age, it's easy to focus too much on our bodies or our emotional lives, behaving as though bulging biceps or endless analysis in themselves could bring us happiness.

It is true that we have bodies and emotions. But we are neither our bodies nor our emotions alone, but a marriage of the two—organized by a wonderful mind, wrapped by a mysterious spirit. In fact, our bodies and minds are so connected that we can even have emotions so powerful that they create changes in our bodies—the depression that drives us to overeat, the unexpressed anger that gives us gall bladder trouble.

We are body, mind, emotions, and spirit, and we need to acknowledge and nurture all the quadrants of our being.

Loving the Mystery

We fall in love with one another for reasons, but beyond the causes we know there is the unknown, unnameable reason, the essence beyond the sum of the parts that draws us inexorably toward one another.

We're often good at knowing, acknowledging, and appreciating the specifics in one another, the attributes we recognize and cherish. But real love gives up on knowing every jot and tittle, stops trying to understand everything.

Real love stands in awe of the ineffable, the part we can't nail down or define. Real love celebrates the mystery, the deep unknowable in another human being.

Develop Consistency

*O*ne of the most underrated attributes of love is consistency, the quality of offering a beautiful sameness, of being able to be counted on, being a person of your word.

When we are consistent we create security for those we love. Against all the randomness of the universe, we establish little islands of steadfastness: the lunch that will always be packed, the note that will always be left, the words of encouragement we can always expect.

When we are consistent, we bring grace to life, make reasonable the quiet hope that some things can indeed be counted on. If you are consistent in what you do, in what you say, in what you give, you are a blessing to everyone around you.

Love, the Infinite

*L*ove will be larger than all your lessons, longer than all your mistakes, sweeter than all the sad sorrows that life will mete out to you.

Love is what matters now; love is what will matter in the end.

Filled to Brimming

*I*t's not only the passion of new romance that teaches us about love, but the substance and content of all of our relationships. It's the sweet moments with our children and their surprising insights; the conflict, tenderness, and forgiving of our parents; the heart-stunning moments of crystalline passion; the ax of grief when a colleague dies; the boundless compassion of lifelong friendships.

All these expand our hearts to brimming, enlarge our souls, and make us the true guardians and the subsequent bestowers of the love with which we have been filled by those who have truly loved us.

The Artistry of Praise

Whenever we acknowledge something that someone has done, when we say, for example, "The words on your birthday card meant so much to me"; "It was beautiful to see the way you embraced your young son"; "I loved hearing you singing behind me in church," we are giving the other person a sense of the meaning of their actions.

Such statements are far more than mere compliments. They are the artisan's tools through which character is formed. For they hold up a mirror for the person who has acted in a particular way and give him a deeper, clearer sense of what he has done. When we praise, we sort out and underline for the other person the meaning and value of his actions, and in so doing we participate with him in sculpting and developing his behavior.

What could be a more remarkable gift from one human being to another!

Johnny-Come-Lately Anger

*T*here's a curious phenomenon that happens with anger. Often, after an irritating behavior has been resolved or eliminated, the person who endured it, rather than being happy and relieved, is suddenly retroactively angry. It's as though the person realizes, "Now that I know you could change this behavior, I'm going to be angry in one big, backward swoop about how long I've had to put up with it before you finally changed."

When you find yourself having this kind of anger, or being the recipient of it, don't be unduly alarmed. It's a passing phenomenon, a little postscript to change—and the sign that something wonderful, something you've hoped for, has finally happened.

So if you need to, indulge your backlash anger a little (or let someone indulge it at you), but not for too long. After all, if you really wanted the change you should be grateful that it's happened.

Truly Receiving

*N*othing gives us a greater sense of our value than having what we have given be received. Therefore, if you wish to show the person you love that he has value, that she is important to you, receive his contributions, accept what she offers.

For whenever you receive what someone gives you, you heal their inner questions of unworthiness. You show them that who they are and what they have offered has merit.

Conversely, when we receive, we not only take in what someone has offered us, we take in the person as well. Truly receiving, therefore, is one of the highest forms of love.

Taking Responsibility

*W*e are responsible for all our actions, whether of thought or behavior, whether deliberate or unintentional. This doesn't mean that we won't make mistakes. What it does mean is that, no matter what, when we have hurt or violated someone we will take responsibility for what we have done.

Whatever the reasons, whatever the extenuating circumstances, whatever the good intentions gone awry, if you didn't call home when you said you would because something kept you late at the office, you didn't call home; if you yelled at your wife because you had too many martinis, you did yell.

Taking emotional responsibility means that rather than blaming, excusing, rationalizing, or trying to fudge about what you did, you make yourself accountable for it, knowing that the person who loves you will recognize your integrity in the acknowledgement and be more than willing to forgive.

Passing through Walls

*L*ove makes us pass through the walls of our own limitations. This means that time and again we find ourselves doing, saying, trying, giving up, or putting up with the very things we swore we never would do, say, or put up with: waiting for him to come home for the 477th time, patiently explaining again why we need time alone....

When we do this for love, we expand not only our horizons but also our boundaries. We become more than we were. We're not always happy about it—frankly, it's a lot of trouble and often it's quite painful—but the lessons we learn make us ever more able to love.

Today, take a look at just one remarkable change you have made because of your absolute utter frustration with someone you love. Celebrate what, because you had to pass through the walls of your limitations, you have become.

Strength Is Self-Love

*S*trength, of whatever form—physical, emotional, sexual, spiritual, intellectual, intuitive—is what delivers us from the tyranny of our past and the limitations we have internalized because of it.

Therefore, strength and the development of it becomes the measure and the mirror of yourself. It delivers you to a larger life, a life of greater dimension and depth. Strength allows you to individuate from your parents, to see your own power, and to use it on your own behalf. Strength is valor, self love that honors your individuality.

Therefore it is important to meditate upon your strengths, to gather the knowledge of them around you like a suit of armor that you have handcrafted yourself, link by link, piece by beautiful piece.

More Praise

*M*any of us are still victims of the antiquated and spirit-withering myth that too much praise is dangerous and could give us a big head. Having not been praised ourselves, we feel shy about praising others, even those we admire and take delight in, as if instead of building their spirits, our praise could ruin them.

But we all need praise—we're starving for it, in fact; and praise, for anything and everything, is one of the buoyant generosities of love.

So praise somebody today—a stranger, a lover, a friend—for who she is, for what he does, for how she speaks, for how he kisses, for what she thinks . . . for how he loves.

Mature Love

We don't always feel like loving the people we're "supposed" to love: our children, our parents, our friends. In fact, every relationship tests us, taxes our spontaneous feelings of love.

Yet it's at the very moment that love stops being a feeling and becomes a responsibility that we are invited to expand and mature. We don't necessarily write our parents a letter because we feel like it; we write because, since they gave us life, we choose to honor them. Nor do we kiss our children at bedtime because, after they've driven us crazy all day, we feel particularly loving. We do it out of duty, because we mean, we intend, we are committed to love them.

Love is a responsibility as well as a sensation, a commitment as well as a feeling; and it is when we can move back and forth between these two diverse but contiguous terrains that we have not only expanded, but truly matured our capacity for loving.

Coming to Peace

*I*n relationships as in life one of our deepest desires is coming to peace, that place with others where we feel our deep connection, our sense of ultimate union.

In our hearts this sense of peace comes in stillness, when we have slowed down our lives and our minds and permitted ourselves to feel the inner silence. But in relationships, where we must work out personal differences and resolve emotional hangovers from the past, coming to peace is much more difficult.

In a relationship, coming to peace begins with believing that, indeed, you can come to peace with the person you love: to comfort, to kindness, to union, and communion. To hold that as a value and to make it one of the highest goals of your relationship is to have already moved a great distance toward achieving it.

Bones of the Earth

We are made of the bones and the dust of the earth. We are part of, and belong to, all that is. We are neither the conquerors, overlords, nor masters of that which is around us. The elements of our bodies and the winds of our spirits are made of the same materials, precisely, as the earth, the stars, and all living things.

To know this is to live on the earth itself, *con amore,* with love, to see it not as a separate entity but as another expression of the stuff of your own being.

As you move through your world today, no matter how far from nature you may seem, remember that the earth is connected to you and that, through the very design of your molecules, you are connected to it.

Tied Up in Knots

*T*ry to remember this the next time a fight has you tied up in knots: The best argument has no winner and nobody gets blamed, for the best argument is a dialogue— heated perhaps, needled with anger no doubt, difficult always—between two people whose positions on a given issue are passionately different.

That two people have different opinions about the same thing is the measure of their uniqueness. That they express their differences is a measure of their courage. That they are willing to listen to someone else's position is a measure of their maturity. And that they are willing to arrive at a solution is a measure of the strength of their relationship.

An argument is a forum, a passionate dialogue, not a battleground or the occasion for a firing squad. And the winner of the truly successful argument is never an individual, but the relationship itself.

Love Is

*L*ove is transcendent experience and daily consolation. What this means is that love is not only high and holy but also cozy and homespun. It's about angels on one hand and slippers on the other. It's about seeing God and it's about not being alone in your bed at night.

Love on either level is not the whole picture nor does it represent all the love we require. We do need to be in the presence of the love that is larger than life, and we need, at the same time, to live and breathe the love that invests our daily lives with simplicity and sweetness.

A Tender Balance

S o often we're focused on developing the strong things in ourselves—becoming tougher, more assertive; developing our potential; learning how to compete and win; rising to the top of the heap—as though our highest goal should be to become the person who can undertake, endure, or withstand anything.

Asking for all this strength in ourselves is a form of emotional denial of the fact that we have been wounded, have weaknesses, are shy or afraid, and possess, along with our capabilities, great areas of fragility, of spiritual brokenness.

Loving yourself isn't asking the impossible or the ridiculous: that willy-nilly you become perfect. Rather, it is living the balance of your brokenness and your wholeness, of your strengths and weaknesses, of your capacity to love, and of your need—no matter how immense or desperate it may seem—to feel that you are loved.

What Gives You Joy?

*L*ife will not, of itself, necessarily grant you joy. Life will give you opportunities and challenges. It will offer you friends and present you with experiences. It will ask you to work and require you to feel, but it will not, necessarily, give you joy.

Joy is a state of the soul, the feeling beyond feeling that allows us to know that it is right to be alive, that our living has meaning and that we belong.

Certain people and experiences, certain spiritual disciplines, some words we utter, certain movements that we make with our bodies, have the capacity to bring us inexplicably and beautifully into the state of immeasurable joy. Today, allow yourself to discover, to seek, and to embrace those things that give you joy.

Thanking the Sun

*T*he sun is the light of our lives. It is the sustenance of life, the mirror of our joy, the source of the light that we are inhabited by.

When the sun is shining our spirits are lifted, exalted by seeing the light. When the sun hides its face, our hearts are exhausted. We need, we feed on the light.

Today, give thanks for the sun: the life, the joy, the power, the source, the eye of God beholding us, in whose light we shine.

To Be Loved

*D*eep inside we all have certain hidden inhibitions and/or restrictions to being loved the way we would really like to be, so much so that at times we can't imagine that being loved is possible.

To break through these barriers, complete the following question. Answer it ten times, until moving through the levels of what you already know, you stumble on the secret which, when you discover it, will allow you to really open up to being loved:

For me to be loved would be _____. (For example: wonderful; scary; impossible; too much the way it was with my father; to have someone hold me and make me feel safe; to get over my lifelong fears of not being loved; to finally come home.)

Enlarge Your Focus

When your attention is constantly focused on the here and now—what you want and need, who's disappointed or hurt you, when your shirts will be ready at the cleaners, or what you're going to have for dinner—life can often seem difficult, wearing, and demanding.

But when you focus on the larger things—the beauty of your consciousness, the meaning of your life, the miracle of the people who have loved you—then everything suddenly seems easy. You know from the inside that everything is perfect, is happening just the way it ought to, and that, even without your attention, your life is following a beautiful pattern.

Love and Only Love

*L*ove is the greatest healing power there is. Nothing comes close to it, not the miracles of modern medicine, not the magic of ancient cures, not the books we read, or what we think and say—although all these things can have a powerful effect on us.

It is love and only love that can fill our hearts, alter our lives, recharge our molecules, transform the very substance of our beings. Love is the light, the life, the gift, the beautifully transforming power in all of us. Nothing can heal like the power of unconditional love.

If you have seen your love as only a feeling or a need, invite yourself now to discover its healing dimension. What can you say or do, with what relaxed judgments, comforting words, or new openness of heart can you approach someone who has been difficult for you? How can you move toward unconditional love?

Your Emotional Work

*I*f you want to love yourself and love others, do your emotional work.

Nothing speeds up the process of personal evolution more than removing our emotional barriers: healing childhood betrayals and abuses, facing what we have suppressed and repressed, dealing with our obsessions, removing our addictions. So long as we are involved with these things we are just that: involved with them. They take our emotional attention; they soak up our energy and time. Resolving these things allows your energies to redirect themselves to higher levels, to other persons.

So if you have nagging little emotional issues that you've been ignoring, or great pains that you've avoided resolving, have courage and deal with them now. Your own soul is waiting for you.

Magical Objects

*O*ur material possessions embody our histories, and remind us, perhaps even more than mere remembering, who we are, where we have been. For this reason, the objects that inhabited your children's lives make wonderful gifts for them in adulthood.

Some of my most treasured possessions—my mother's prayer book, the crystal from my father's watch—and my daughter's—the poems I wrote the week she was born, the wooden angels she got every Christmas—are valuable not because of their material worth but because they are symbols of a whole relationship, talismans of a life-shaping love.

No matter how ordinary or even worthless a particular object may be, it can hold a message that touches your heart. So cherish the objects that carry these messages for you, and retain for your children the objects that have the power to carry the messages for them.

Our True Survival

When we really love ourselves we nourish ourselves, not only our bodies but, more importantly, our spirits. What this means is that we understand that there is more to us, more to our true survival than merely keeping ourselves physically alive.

We each have a mysterious part—the part that shines through our eyes, that moves us to love one another, that we feel without words—and this essence also needs to be nourished.

The spirit is nourished in silence, in nature, in the presence of other spirits, in the calming reflections of water, by music, by carefully chosen words.

Take a moment today to consciously nourish your spirit.

Give It Away

Whatever you possess will become most truly yours only when you give it away.

If you have a talent, it will become visible because you use it; if you have financial resources, their power will become obvious because you share them; if you have words of wisdom, their value will become apparent because you have delivered them to the world; if you have beauty, you will discover it because it brings joy to those around you. Whatever is yours will become enlarged in your perception through its power to change, heal, or delight the people with whom you share it.

If you have a talent, give it away. Then it will become truly yours.

Imagine the Life

*I*magine the life you desire. Who shares it with you? What do you do in it? How do you spend your time day by day, during the week, and on weekends?

Whom do you talk to? What are your rooms like? What special things do you do for yourself?

How is the life you imagine unlike the life you live now? What, starting today, can you change so that tomorrow you will be one step closer to living the life of your dreams?

Your Own Beauty

*S*ometimes we feel as though it's a crime to celebrate ourselves, to authentically acknowledge our gifts, to take possession of our special attributes. Owning your beauty, allowing yourself to acknowledge the truth about the gifts that you uniquely possess, is one of the healing practices of an appropriate self-love.

This doesn't mean that you should go around always tooting your own horn, making a spectacle of your wonderful self. What it does mean is that from the inside, deeply, truly, and with unshakable conviction, you will recognize your gifts, and that as you move through life, you will operate from this quiet knowledge.

So if you have been prevented from holding the truth about your own beauty, allow yourself to discover it now, for the beauty you own in yourself is the beauty with which, as time goes on, you will bless all those who pass through your life.

AUGUST 21

Becoming a Mirror

*B*eing a mirror is one of the greatest gifts you can give to the person you love. In being a mirror, we hold up an image so that our beloved can finally, accurately, and wonderfully, capture an image of him or herself.

Deciding to be a mirror takes effort and love and attention. Here we consciously choose to show the person to himself: through compliments (you are beautiful), through listening (you sound sad), through observation (you're different from your sisters), through contemplation (I sense something, but its meaning hasn't come clear to me yet), through the pure expression of love (I love you; I will love you always).

Today, allow yourself to become a mirror, and let your mirroring become a sweet reflection of your love.

Seeing the Pattern

*T*here are times in our lives when, momentarily, we are illumined. We see that everything follows a pattern and that the pattern fits together beautifully.

We don't always feel this way of course. We all occasionally have "one of those days," but we also have days, moments, and hours in which we see that all the right things have happened, that our lives have unfolded just as they should, that we have been given just what we needed.

This kind of seeing is recognizing the pattern, and this recognition is knowing that, at the center, everything is connected, is tied together by love.

Carpe Diem

*T*oday, seize the moment—to make love, to go swimming in the river, to give the magic surprise, to say the beautiful touching words, to hold hands while you sleep, to say "You are the most unbelievable miracle of my life."

Today, seize the moment. For the moment passes like the river and is gone.

Stop Feeding Your Fears

*O*ur fears are like a bunch of mad dogs crouched outside the gates of our lives, wildly barking and howling.

Don't feed the mad dogs of your fears by turning them over and over again in your mind, asking "What if?" or "What now?" Indulging your fears is like throwing food to the dogs, making them bigger and stronger, inviting them to growl louder, bark longer.

Instead, treat your fears like visiting dignitaries. They're here on a mission, although its purpose may still be uncertain and you're not quite sure how to deal with them. Give them the proper respect. Know that their visit has limits—they'll leave when their business is finished—and meanwhile pay careful attention, so that you won't ever have to entertain them unnecessarily again.

Receive the Gift!

A gift not received becomes a tragedy. If you have something you really want to give and for some reason the recipient is unable to appropriately receive it, you are left, as it were, holding the bag.

We all need to feel loving as well as to be loved and one of the ways to experience this is through giving. What we have to offer may literally be a gift or it may be the contribution of our professional expertise, our financial resources, our wisdom, or our wonderful gourmet cooking.

When our gifts are not received, we feel rejected, strangely gray and useless, as though our love isn't good enough, as though we can't have impact.

Thus receiving is, in a sense, a gift in itself. So look for the place in yourself that can truly take in what has been given to you. Give the gift of receiving.

Your Immense Fragility

*I*n each of us there is an immense fragility, a soul-deep softness, a subtlety of emotion and delicacy of spirit that longs to be expressed and intricately responded to. When we deny the fragility in ourselves, we also deny it in others. As a result we often create relationships that are conducted on an emotionally unsatisfying level.

When we acknowledge our fragility, however, our internal tenderness, we discover the deeply touching, eternally moving, and awesomely beautiful aspects of love. So for a moment today, honor your own intense fragility, the exquisiteness of your spirit, the refinement of your emotions, the depth of your desire to be loved. And know that because you have honored your own fragility, in time it will be honored by others in return.

A Meditative Moment

*G*ive yourself time today in silence and aloneness. Something deeper and truer will be revealed to you.

Cherish All As Children

We are gradually coming to understand that children are the most abused minority. In relation to parents, they have no ultimate power to express or defend themselves or to fulfill their own interests. They can be done to, taken from, used and abused according to their parents' whims. They have no protection whatsoever except their parents' emotional maturity.

While they are children, they can't improve their situation. Because they lack the maturity—the language, perception, objectivity, and power—that could alter their circumstances, they are truly at our mercy. If you're a parent now, it's important to keep this in mind.

And if you're not a parent you need to remember that inside every adult, no matter how strong he or she may appear, is a small love-deprived child. Only the love you give now can make up for the love he or she didn't get then.

A Bridge to Intimacy

*E*xpressing anger can be an act of intimacy. When we identify it and deliver it in a loving way, we become connected to some of our oldest pains. For anger is always attached to places where we have been hurt. Thus in showing our anger, we expose old wounds.

"I'm angry because you didn't finish the fence. You made me feel unworthy—the way I felt with my father. He always promised but never finished anything."

If we can express the old root of our anger, instead of having the anger be a divisive explosion, we unbandage some of our tenderest places, reveal our most vulnerable selves.

So when you're angry, don't just express your current complaint. Try also to tell its history, what happened to make you so sensitive now. That way, instead of being the nasty abyss that separates you two, your anger can be a bridge to true intimacy.

Prepare for Love

*I*n order to receive love, you need to know what love consists of for you. Just holding the vague hope that you'll "get loved" or that you'll "fall in love" isn't enough. Our experience of love is very specific. We feel loved when we receive exactly the kind of love that speaks to us.

So today, if you are seeking love or desire to feel more love, ask yourself the following questions: What would the person who loves me look like? How would he or she speak to me? How would he or she touch me, move, behave, in the presence of my body?

What are the words she would say? What are the things I would need him to tell me? What, most of all, would we enjoy doing together? Why would she love me? What would be the reasons he or she has chosen me to love?

More Will Be Revealed

Sometimes when we're stuck in a particularly difficult place it feels as though nothing has, or ever will, change. At such moments we need encouragement for our spirits, a way of looking at what feels impossible in a new and encouraging light.

This is the time to tell yourself that more will be revealed, that what you see now is not the whole picture. What will occur in the future is not what's happening now; even the meaning of what you're going through now will, with the passage of time, be changed and amplified.

So if you're discouraged, if it seems like you're stuck—in a situation, with a person, with a puzzle—just quietly tell yourself that where you are now isn't where you'll end up. For more, most certainly, will be revealed.

The Power of Your Words

What we say to one another, the tenderness with which we reveal our hopes and disappointments and unveil our dreams and fears, the language with which we complain and ask for comfort or forgiveness, the phrases with which we encourage, the sentences with which we negotiate, the care with which we choose our words—all these are the ways we bond ourselves through language.

Language, conveying particular meaning through specifically ordered arrangements of sounds, is a peculiarly human ability. Through our words, what we say and the care with which we deliver them, we can enhance or diminish, create or destroy our experience of love.

Do It Right Now

*T*he beautiful things you want to say to the person you love, say them now; the walks you want to take on the beach but think you don't have time for, take them now; the conversations that come from your heart, the sorrows you need to share, the shoulder you want to offer your sweetheart to cry on, offer it now.

Time is so fast and life is so short; you and your darling won't be here forever. So long as we're here, as human beings loving each other, we need to say the words, have the fun, do the things, give the gifts, open our hearts, console one another. Time isn't forever.

Whatever it is, do it *now*.

The Smallest Change

When we feel as though our relationships are at a standstill, we're often immediately discouraged: things are the way they are; we don't know what to do so we feel like giving up.

If this is where you find yourself, here's a quick fix. Look for one tiny thing you could do that would immediately in some way alter the situation. Not starting over, not giving up, not turning the world upside down, but the smallest change that would make the biggest difference: having some help four hours a week, sending out the shirts instead of doing all the laundry, making sure you have a Friday night date together instead of always losing out on intimate time.

Problems usually aren't solved by bucketfuls; they're solved by teaspoonfuls. So today look for—and enact—the smallest change that could make the biggest difference.

How Do You Feel?

*M*ost of us don't know how we feel at any given moment and hence we conduct our lives in ways that hurt us, disappoint us, wheel us off in directions we had never meant to go, or unwittingly put us in the position of hurting others.

To begin to tune in, ask yourself how you feel: about your work, about the person you're most closely related to, about your child, about your best friend.

Think of one thing you're angry about, and one thing you're delighted by in each of these categories, and you will have begun to discover, uncover, and recover your life. Rather than life controlling you, you will be able to start to reshape life around what you really feel.

The Near Side of the Wall

*T*here's a place some of us like to hang out; I call it the near side of the wall. It's the comfortable place where, instead of pushing our limits to more intense feeling, greater love, and larger life, we remain content with half best, with mediocrities in every area, with things that fill our days but not our souls.

Playing on the near side of the wall is at best a timid and at worst a cowardly position. It ensures that our lives will be safe and small.

Being willing to climb over the wall, to scale it in spite of possible bruised hands and scraped knees, is like being willing to see if the baseball you threw over it ended up on a black-asphalt pavement or in a field of wild orange poppies.

The Gift of Perception

*P*erception, the ability to see another person clearly, is one of the rarest talents around. We don't all have this talent, and even to the degree that we do, our ability to use it is often limited because of our own emotional problems.

If we're scared, we can't see; if we wonder about our own value, we can't see; if we're healing from abuse, we're also often unable to clearly perceive another human being.

Therefore, if you want to really notice and respond to another person, make it your business to clear your own emotional screen. Deal with whatever blocks you from seeing, so you can give the gift of perception.

SEPTEMBER 7

The Needs Wish List

*E*xpressing your own needs and responding to somebody else's is an important function of any loving relationship. But often we're so out of touch with our needs that we can't even figure out what they are, much less express them or know the joy of having them met.

A need represents something you don't already have, an empty slot on your dance card of life, something without which you suffer and through the fulfillment of which you are enhanced.

But you can't have your needs met unless you know what they are; so today, even though it may be scary, strange, and unfamiliar, allow yourself to identify three very specific things that you need—in whatever area of your life—and know that identifying them will be the beginning of getting them fulfilled.

Go for It

When you take risks, you "go for it." You take a stand at the core of your being, project it out into the world, and are willing to take the consequences—even when at points along the way the thing you hoped for confronts you with disappointment.

Taking risks creates results. Ambivalence doesn't. Passivity doesn't. Waiting and seeing doesn't. Even leaving it all up to God won't do it in itself; for we participate in creating the world, the life we live, the air we breathe. Even with God on our side, it's the risks we're willing to take in pursuing our intentions we express that will ultimately create the fulfillment of our dreams.

Body and Spirit

Some of us think of our bodies as not what we are, and others believe our bodies are all that we are. In each of these extremes we miss the mystical, magical marriage of our bodies and spirits.

To think of yourself as not a body is to miss the point of incarnation—that you have been given life in a physical form and that the expression of yourself, your essence, through the movements, gestures, speakings, healings, feelings, sensations, and responses of your body is one of the highest expressions of being human.

To think of yourself as only a body is to miss the depth that the life of the spirit conveys and to live separated from the deepest communion you can have with other human beings. Invite your spirit to marry your body, and you will enjoy the highest experience of incarnation.

The Sustenance of Consistency

*C*onsistency is the steadiness of love, the ongoing sameness that can be endlessly, beautifully counted upon. It isn't glamorous; it isn't particularly exciting; it doesn't give you a buzz. But knowing she'll always do what she says; knowing he'll always come home on time; knowing the children will get their allowance, week after week, month after month; knowing she'll be there to kiss you good night is the grounding, the foundation, of a life-sustaining love.

Consistency may not be as wildly exciting as passion, hysteria, or raging discontent, but against the undercurrent of its steadiness the exceptions and variations of life can be comfortably played out.

Consistency is the cornerstone, the deep sustenance of love.

Love Dispels Fear

When you are in the midst of love—feeling love, making love, giving love—fear vanishes. Nothing you have ever worried about can hold court in your consciousness when it is consumed with love. Love takes up all the psychic, emotional, and spiritual space. When love is with you, there isn't room for anything else.

When we are "in love" and we feel fear, we have for a moment stepped away from our deepest connection with love. Old fears and historical insecurities have wormed their way into our consciousness, displacing the love that in our purest state we can readily feel. But at the core of ourselves, we need to let go of fear to hold on to love.

Healing Miracle

*E*motional healing is one of the most powerful consequences of true love. It is the miracle that occurs when,
in the presence of the person who loves you now, you are
able to say what you were unable to say as a child and to
express and complete the aspects of yourself that were suppressed, ignored, or degraded when you were too little to
protect yourself.

Emotional healing is the primary function of our intimate relationships. We may think that security is, or companionship, or play, but whether we consciously attend to it
or not, emotional healing is always going on. We heal and
change one another profoundly because of our relationships.

Making Merry

*M*aking merry is making sure life isn't all work and no play, that Jack is not a dull boy.

To make merry is to make sure that sometime, more often than you have been, you pause in the midst of the fracas and fray of your daily routine to paint your toenails gold or to bring home some balloons for no important reason.

Create occasions. Make ridiculous reasons for celebrations. Be frivolous, carefree, and happy. Making merry makes life much lighter and sweeter, a carnival, a festival. So whenever you can, make merry.

SEPTEMBER 14

Melting the Boundaries

*L*ove is a melting of the boundaries. Through it we enter one another's bodies, hearts, and minds. We sense another human spirit; we partake of the human condition.

We hear so much these days about overinvolvement with others, about the need to have strong boundaries; and indeed boundaries are appropriate much of the time. So how do we differentiate between love and invasion?

When the melting of boundaries flatters our spirits, enhances us, and makes us feel whole, we are experiencing love; when the dissolution of boundaries makes us fearful, gives us a sense of having been wrongly encroached upon, we are being invaded, abused. Just as we have had to be vigilant about developing our boundaries, so too must we be passionate in allowing love to dissolve the barriers that we have built so we can let more love flow in.

Feeling Is Being Alive

*F*eeling, feeling everything: that's the point of life. And the more you allow yourself to experience the endlessly undulating and exquisite variations of feelings, the more exquisitely alive you will find yourself to be. Feeling is living; the absence of feeling is death.

Healthy Self-Focus

Sometimes we think we should avoid the indulgence of self-focus: thinking too much about our own problems and goals, worrying about our own feelings, feeling sorry for ourselves, needing things. It is possible, of course, to become overly self-involved, and we all know people who exhaust us by doing this. But taking the time to really know yourself, in a sweet and intricate way, is a holy undertaking, the beginning of self-love.

Getting acquainted with your hurts, allowing yourself to remember and re-feel the words and experiences that shaped your life, that formed your gifts, and developed your limitations—this is the process of self-knowing that allows you to view your own soul with tender compassion. And in the end this process becomes the vehicle by which you are also able to love and consider others.

Entrusted to You

*I*n each of us there are incredibly beautiful gifts, not only capabilities for us to enjoy, but qualities and attributes with which we can also bless others.

The remarkable qualities you have—intelligence, physical strength, perseverance, lightness of spirit, sturdiness of character, whatever they are—imply responsibility. They haven't been given to you just to indulge yourself; they have been entrusted to you to discover, develop, and share with all the rest of us.

Therefore honor your gifts and be responsible for them. Tell yourself the truth about their nature and magnitude, and look for the avenues through which, as your life progresses, you can share them with the world.

The Architecture of Feeling

W hen we take note of how we feel—what angers and disappoints us, what moves us deeply, what brings back an old sorrow, what delights us and make us feel like kite-flying children again—we ever so delicately begin to restructure our reality along different lines.

When we know what we love, what brings us joy, and especially when we start to pay attention to these feelings, on an unconscious level we gradually begin to draw the things that please us into our lives. Conversely, when we know what scares and hurts us, we gradually draw away from those things. In this way, even without willpower or serious conscious intention we begin to create lives that more and more feed and delight us.

So allow yourself to know what you feel; your emotions are the structural beams of a truly beautiful life.

No Choice But Forgiveness

*N*o matter how far along you may be on your spiritual path, the truth about your capacity to love will be excruciatingly revealed in how you feel after a fight with your sweetheart. In forgiving him, in accepting her for who she really is, you will be called upon by love to become the highest and best self you can be. This doesn't always feel good. In fact, it often feels better to be our petty, back-biting, unevolved selves. But love asks better of us; and because we also need to be loved, love makes us learn to forgive.

What crummy little resentment are you still holding on to? Take it out of your knapsack and express it today. In working it through, in receiving your darling back into your heart, you will see that your forgiveness of him or her is also a homecoming for you.

Ecstatic Energy

*L*ove reorganizes our consciousness. It revises our notions of how things are and carries us up on the power of its own ecstatic energy, inviting us to revise our perceptions of almost everything.

Just when we're sure that we know how things are, love comes along and upends us: "I don't like men with brown hair, but I've fallen in love with a brown-haired man"; "I don't like tall women, but I'm falling head over heels for a woman who's six feet tall."

Love shows us that love is stronger than we thought, believed, or imagined. Love makes us give up our little self-centered controlling notions of how life is and ought to be. Love makes us change, against our will, for the better. If you're not convinced, think for a minute how many times love has gotten your goat or made you eat your own words.

Too Much of a Good Thing?

*I*n a healthy relationship, both people feel as though the other person gets his or her way too much of the time. This isn't a sign of dysfunction, but of the fact that there are two individuals here, each one aware of his or her needs and also of when these needs don't get met.

The truth is, when we're generous-spirited people, we often feel taken advantage of in relationships. But when you love someone who loves you generously in return, you'll find out—if you bother to check—that at times he or she feels taken advantage of too.

Take some time today to talk to the person you love about the areas in which you feel you've given too much. Then let him or her do the same. You'll find that out of a total 100, you're probably both giving 90 percent.

Closing the Circle

*T*here's a certain point in life where parents, as parents, become irrelevant. To know this as a parent, and to release your children so they can conduct their own lives, is the paramount act of parental love. As a child, to recognize that your parents have had the grace to do this is to experience the moment of maturation in your relationship with them.

If you're a parent—or a child—ask yourself if this moment has arrived in your life. What are the signs if it has? If it hasn't, how can you prepare yourself for it? How can you thank your parents (or your children) for closing this special circle of your bondedness—the days when you were so sweetly con-nected—with such parental grace?

Cultivating Self-Esteem

What psychologists call "self-esteem" is, very simply, the amount of good that we are able to believe about ourselves. If we believe a lot of good things we are said to have healthy self-esteem; if we believe a lot of bad things we are said to have low self-esteem.

Whatever we may still need to discover about ourselves—how artistic, smart, or good-natured we are—we all have certain beliefs about ourselves that form our core sense of who we are. And we can build upon this knowledge to eventually gain a true sense of self-value.

Today, before you dismiss yourself as a person who has a problem with self-esteem, make a list of all the good things you already know about yourself. Use this as the basis for developing an awareness of all the other wonderful things that are part of your essence. Eventually, you will develop a true sense of self-esteem, a complete and accurate picture of yourself.

Affected by Love

When we love someone, we allow them to have impact on us, to affect us, to encourage us in one direction or another. We change our wardrobes and hair. We travel. We give up bad habits. We do things we were scared to do before. And we do all these things not because someone asked or demanded but because in his presence, by her example, we feel naturally inclined to change. In fact we often change without quite noticing we have.

What are the changes the people who love you have generated in your life? And how can you thank them for the happy consequences of their love?

In a Positive Way

I have a friend who, no matter when you ask him what he is doing, will say: "I'm generally moving through life in a positive way."

To generally move through life in a positive way is to live in a state of grace, of love, expecting that life will bring you remarkable surprises, and knowing that your effect on life will be as gracious as its effect on you.

To move through life in a generally positive way is not only an attitude or an expectation; it is a prayer of thanksgiving to the universe for the pleasure of being alive.

The Garden of Friendship

*F*riendships are like a spiritual garden. In the rich soil of our lives they bloom like many beautiful flowers. They have different qualities and colors; we pick them for a variety of reasons. They are the calla lilies at our mournings, the extravagant long-stemmed red roses at our romantic celebrations, the wild clover and the black-eyed susans in the background of our lives, quietly leafing, budding, and blooming.

Over a lifetime we gather many blossoms from the garden of our friendships, knowing that they will nourish our spirits. For they are the steady meadow of flowers among which the strong stalks of our own lives can reach for the sun and bloom.

The Medium of Connection

We each have a special means through which we relate to those we love. You may relate to your mother through going shopping together, your teenaged son through watching sports, your husband through working in the garden. Whatever this medium is, it is the special channel through which you conduct your relationship. It probably has something to do with what brought you together in the first place, and it certainly reveals the point to which you should return whenever you lose your footing and need to regain your bearings.

The medium of connection is your safe place, your unique way of being together. To know it is to nurture it, to allow it to serve you even more, to be grateful that whatever disasters or little divisivenesses befall you, you have a stronghold of connection that you can always count on.

The Art of Consolation

*O*ne of our most difficult tasks as loving human beings is to provide consolation. To console is to join company with, to bond in the hour of suffering. Consoling is being willing to enter in at the depth of the wound. It is to participate in another's sorrow by offering your hand.

Consolation is a spiritual undertaking. It begins with the recognition that from time to time we all suffer, and proceeds to the conviction that it is our duty to commiserate with one another when we do. Consolation is not, however, morbid; it operates on the principle that light can be brought into darkness, that what we have to offer can be received, that our love can make a difference.

Offering yourself is itself the art of consolation. So if someone around you is suffering, give them your hand. The hand of your hand, the hand of your words, the hand of your time, the hand of your heart.

Unconditional—and Conditional—Love

*U*nconditional love is translucent total acceptance, the love that not only sees perfection in the imperfect human being, but is totally willing to accept the other as is. This is the love that, ideally, parents should give to their children, the love that we want to be able to give to all those we love. This is love in a spiritual dimension.

But in a real live relationship, love has conditions. We will not—nor should we—endlessly forgive, accept, overlook, or ignore behaviors that wound and violate us. Love on this level—conditional love—has requirements. It asks, through the conscious imposition of standards, that the persons we love—and we ourselves—act with integrity, move from the truth, and be all that we can.

Relationship as Process

A relationship is a process, not a destination. It is a holy interpersonal environment for the evolution of two souls, an experience of the evolution of your individual consciousness in the presence of another human being whose consciousness is also evolving.

We must resist the temptation to define relationships as anything less than this: the absolutely most powerful tools we have for our spiritual evolution.

Asking for What You Want

*A*sking for what you want from your beloved is one of the conditions of getting loved. If you don't ask and she's not a mind reader, the chances of getting what you want become infinitesimal.

Asking of course requires knowing what you want so that you can ask. And knowing what you want also includes being aware of what you don't want—the kinds of behaviors that hurt, irritate, or offend you. Telling your sweetheart what pleases you and what doesn't is precisely the communication that can strengthen the bonds of your relationship.

So take a risk today by telling the person you love exactly what you want and don't want. Then return the favor by asking him, "What would you like me to give you?" And, perhaps, even more important, "What would you like me to refrain from doing around you?"

Make It Your Business

Our capacity to love is limited to the degree that we have not resolved our emotional problems. When we have hidden emotional issues we are constantly occupied with them, both consciously and unconsciously. Questions such as "Am I OK?", cauldrons of unexpressed, unidentified anger, fears that inhibit life movement—all these take up not only our energy and time, but also the pure free emotion with which, if we were liberated, we could love.

Therefore make it your business to do your emotional work. Unfinished emotional business, more than anything else, stands in the way of loving and really being loved.

At the Center

*L*ove is at the heart of every action, interaction, relationship, need, conflict, resolution, endeavor, possibility, and outcome in life. We move toward love. We live for love. Love is our breath, our goal, our source, and our best medicine.

Love is the sound between the sounds, the eye in the midst of the seeing. Love is who we are and how we are and why we came to be.

Today—and always—remember that love is at the center of you. Of everything.

Part of the Fabric

O ver time our friendships become so intricately woven into our lives, so much a part of the fabric of our days, that we often forget just how they began, how much we rely on them, how incredibly much they mean to us.

If romance is the tightrope from which, bespangled, we dance and survey the whole circus, then friendship is the safety net into which we fall whenever, momentarily, we lose our footing.

Today, take time to acknowledge the friendships that, more than once, have kept you from falling in a crumpled heap on the big-top floor.

The Realm of the Senses

S exuality becomes an evermore beautiful vocabulary when we allow it to include sensuality. Sensuality is the delicious gratuitousness of making love, the unnecessary but wonderful play of all the senses—touch, sight, smell, hearing, and taste.

Expressing sensuality is an elevation of our interaction, an invitation for us to become more fully human, to live from our instinctual sensing selves as well as our rational thinking selves. When we make love through the richness of our sensuality, we receive the body of our beloved in the whole complexity of his or her incarnation.

By being generous with our own sensuality, with our beautifully intoxicating words, beholding the gracefulness of the body we cherish, breathing in its fragrance, tasting its essence, we nourish one another's souls.

OCTOBER 6

Your Darling

*Y*our darling is the person you love most in the world, the one you adore, the one who brings you flowers or cooks you banana nut pancakes, who wipes your tears, who plays with you, who cares.

Your darling is your sweetheart, your honey, your mate, your partner, your very own "my dear."

Today, cherish your darling, whatever you call her. Give thanks for your darling; be ever so glad he is here.

Knowing It All

Self-righteousness is "knowing it all," being sure that you're right. You know how it is; you know how it should be, how everybody should do it, and why they should do it the way that you're so sure they should.

Self-righteousness is judgment, pure and simple, of others and, less visibly, of ourselves. For when we are self-righteous what we're really revealing is that we don't really feel terrific about ourselves. For some reason we think we should know more than we do, and we compensate for our fear of not knowing by acting as though we know everything.

So if self-righteousness is your bag, ask yourself what it is that you can't accept in yourself, why you can't forgive yourself for not knowing it all. Then get off the bench, throw in the gavel, and start letting everyone else be good enough just as they are.

Spot Check

*T*oday take your emotions one level deeper by doing a little emotional check-in. Ask yourself the following questions:

Who am I complaining about that I need to get angry at?

Who am I angry at that I need to forgive?

Who am I unable to forgive?

What would I need to change in myself in order to forgive her or him?

In Sickness and in Health

*L*ove calls on us to be with those we love in sickness and in health. We know how to love one another in times of well-being, but when sickness strikes we often feel inadequate. Going through a difficult illness is, of course, scary and terrible for the person who is sick, but it is also an extraordinary burden for those who stand on the sidelines because, often, they don't know how to behave.

You need to know these things: The sickness in the person you love will bring out a variety of feelings in you—sympathy, empathy, fear, and, perhaps most surprising, anger. You will be angry about being scared, and you will be angry about all the burdens that illness imposes. Try to be honest with yourself about your negative feelings so you can be generous with the person who needs your love more than ever. And believe that you can honor your pledge of in sickness and in health.

Your Emotional Truth

*E*xpressing your emotional truth is an act of self-affirmation. Saying how you feel, what you need, what hurts, what you want and hope for—even in the face of possible criticism or rejection, even if you feel vulnerable—is your acknowledgement to yourself and others that your inner experience is valid, worthy of being expressed.

When you communicate your emotional truth, you assert your right to have your inner life have an impact on your outer world. In this way you can sculpt your relationships so they fulfill your needs and delight your heart.

What emotional truth do you need to express today?

Self-Treasuring

Self-love is more than self-tolerance, just putting up with yourself. It is a deeply registered sense of the unrepeatable essence that is you. It is a celebration of your inviolate uniqueness—not only of your graces and perfections, but also of the sorrows, tragedies, and limitations that have shaped you.

Today allow yourself to consciously consider how truly special you are. Why do you love yourself? What it is about you that everyone loves that they've never noticed in anyone else? What is the sorrow, the bearing of which has beautifully formed your character?

Take a good look at yourself. Give yourself a healthy dose of a soul-healing potion of self-love, for self-love steps across the drawbridge of mere self-acceptance and dances into the castle of compassionate self-treasuring.

Little Insecurity Monsters

We all have rattling little insecurities that make us behave somewhat badly in love—the fear of being abandoned, the fear that we're not enough, to name just two. When we feel insecure we try to control—by threatening and bossing, by being mean, by becoming overly possessive.

We all have insecurities but they don't just disappear at will. The way to handle them isn't by becoming controlling or hysterical. When you feel small and inadequate, talk about it, be open about what you're afraid of so that the person you love, instead of feeling abused and controlled, can shower you with the reassurance you need.

What little insecurity monsters are nibbling at you? What fears do you need to reveal to the person you love?

Loving Compromise

*E*very relationship requires a certain amount of renouncing, setting aside, or reconfiguring of our desires in order to complement the needs, desires, and circumstances of the person to whom we are related.

We don't always like to do this and we can become extremely resentful about it. But the cruel fact is that we have to. For a necessary component of every relationship is compromise; otherwise, unless you're in love with a clone of yourself, you literally couldn't live with anyone else.

This compromising is made easier if we realize that the very act of setting aside our own preferences and doing the thing she wants, he prefers, is one of the most important ways we love one another.

So indulge him; give her what she wants. This isn't losing ground; it's being loving.

Being Nice

*B*eing nice means just that—making an effort, looking for the emotional state of grace that will allow you to be thoughtful and kind instead of crabby, surly, short-tempered, cocky, sarcastic, critical, condescending, or pontifical.

Being nice is neither a truly elevated nor a particularly denigrating state. Rather it is the expression of a good-spirited emotional equilibrium, a finding and keeping of the middle ground that will allow you to be gracious, good-natured, and considerate.

In general, it's not very hard to be nice, but some days it's more difficult than others. So when you're tempted by the crabby bug, try to remember that being nice is the lowest common denominator of any sweet relationship.

Out on a Limb

*F*rom time to time in your relationship with a brother or sister, colleague or friend, child, or lover, you will observe an incident or pattern of behavior that is somehow destructive or damaging. Your best friend lets her child run out of control; your brother is endlessly sarcastic to his wife; your boss belittles her secretary. What, as a loving person, should you do?

This is always a very delicate question. Should you speak up, go out on a limb—"I'm disturbed about the way you treat Susie Q"—or should you ignore that person's limitations in his or her capacity to love?

Going out on a limb takes courage—and diplomacy. Be sure you check your own motives, then speak very gently, but directly, about the problem. Confronting someone lovingly about their unlovingness is a very loving thing to do.

On a Lark

When I was a little girl, my father used to say when things were getting too serious that we should "go on a lark." This meant taking the trolley out to the end of the line and exploring an unfamiliar neighborhood, going for a walk on the stones in the creek instead of on the path alongside it, or visiting a junk shop and coming home with a worthless trinket to commemorate our jaunt.

Going on a lark is an undertaking that is meaningless in itself, but it takes on a magical aura because it breaks the bounds of the usual, because it's silly and pointless, because you do it with someone you love.

Today, or soon, go on a lark.

With Caring

Sometimes we get very bogged down in love, constricted or overinvolved in what we should do for each other: You do the dishes and I'll make the dinner; You take out the trash and I'll fix the dryer; It's your turn to help Johnny with his homework because I did it yesterday.

We can get so busy trying to handle and sort out everything that we forget the basic down-home common denominator of any good relationship—simple caring.

Caring is holding a quiet inner concern for the person you love. It is less specific yet more emotionally connecting than any of the multitude of particulars we actually do for one another. Caring is the matrix, the ground from which the particulars spring. Whatever you do for your darling, whatever obligations or favors, do them with caring.

The Beauty of Risk

*T*aking emotional risks, talking about how you feel, admitting to caring for or having hopes about the person you are dating, revealing a silly old hurt, confessing to a physical insecurity—all these may seem like the infinitesimal increments of self-disclosure, and indeed they are. But each one of these has a gigantic power, the power to move your relationship from the emotional shallows to the depths of passionate intimacy.

What are some little disclosures you can make, a few fragile hopes that you can reveal? How can you take the emotional risks that will re-create and deepen your love?

To Have Integrity

*I*ntegrity is the state of holding your own spiritual center. It means that at the core what you do and what you believe are intertwined in such a way that they not only symbolize but are also expressive of one another.

To have integrity is to be a person of quality, to represent through your words and behavior, the truths you believe, the values embodied by your highest thinking and clearest seeing. When we have integrity, we can be trusted—by others and by ourselves. We know that what we offer in all our relationships is unmarred by sloppiness, untruths, or impurity.

When we have integrity, we have peace in ourselves; and we bring peace to others.

Naming Our Wounds

We all have great wounds from our parents, wounds that have shaped our lives. Our wounds represent not only our disabilities, but through the alchemy of time and healing, also the contributions we have to make to the world.

However, we are unable to use our talents or to enjoy ourselves unless and until we have understood the nature and the depth of our wounds, how we are scarred by them, and what strengths in us the scarring has created.

To name your wound is to know it and to enter into the process of its healing. Therefore today ask yourself the question and answer it from deep in your soul: What is the name of the wound from my mother? What is the name of the wound from my father? Naming the wounds is the beginning of healing.

The Pain of Love

*I*t's painful to be around great love, whether that's the love you observe or the love you receive. For love brings us into the presence of feelings so intense—of longing, of hope, of dreaming and wishing—that at times they can be almost overwhelming.

Love never lets us vegetate, simply lie back and soak up the goodies. It asks us to see who we are, to be bigger and more, to become who, in the original infinite and eternal pattern, we were intended to be.

So if you feel the pain of love, don't be confused and imagine that your love is wrong or that its only truth is pain. For the pain is the knots on the backside of the tapestry of love that have as their counterparts on the front side an exquisitely beautiful pattern.

The Wings of Love

*L*ove is the wings that will carry us from life to light. Love is what makes living possible and dying bearable, both our own death and the saddening departures of all those whom we have cared about.

For it is love and only love that bridges the abyss between life as we have known it and life as we shall discover it after death. Whatever love we feel, give, discover, or receive in this life, that love is the pattern, the prototype, and the window to the inestimable radiant, pure, incomprehensible love we shall feel in the light after light after life.

Graciousness to Yourself

When we are depleted, empty, or overdrawn, we have nothing left with which to give to others. Our capacity both to give and receive is suddenly very quietly amputated. We want to withdraw, to remove ourselves from the flow of the human stream. But in this isolation not only are we ourselves robbed, we also rob others from the joy of their experience of us.

Taking care of yourself, being nourished and replenished is not, as we sometimes imagine, a matter of self-indulgence. It is the graciousness to one human being—yourself—that is the source of your graciousness to all others.

Keep the Faith

*K*eeping the faith is expecting a positive outcome even when all the signs—he didn't call, the letter didn't arrive—seem to point in another direction.

Keeping the faith is trusting you are loved, even if at the moment you lack the evidence. It's believing that the person who loves you will not just stop loving you out of the blue, with no warning whatsoever. Keeping the faith is holding the position that there must be a good reason why he hasn't called, why she forgot to write. Perhaps the plane was delayed, perhaps the letter was returned in error.

Keeping the faith is not about holding unrealistic hopes; rather it is the willingness to give the benefit of the doubt. Keeping the faith requires effort. It is an act of believing you are loved. And that belief in itself will increase your chances of discovering that you are.

In Generosity

Generosity is one of the hallmarks of a loving person. Generosity is doing more than is necessary, keeping an open heart, not measuring the consequences, and operating from the expectation that you will not have been a fool for having been so easy with your resources, whatever they are.

For the most part, we're all too stingy with our resources, afraid that we'll give too much and regret it afterward. But it really is true that the more you give, the more you get.

So cultivate your generosity. Be generous with your money, with your time, with your words, with your body. Be a generous friend, lover, sweetheart; be a generous parent, a generous child. You will fill the lives of others and will be rewarded yourself by the recognition of the riches from which you have to give.

A Magical Person

*F*rom time to time into each of our lives there steps a magical person. Out of nowhere, seemingly for no reason, a human being appears whose romance with life is so beautiful and rare, so whimsical and holy that, without any effort at all, he enchants us with his extraordinary gift for living.

Such people are life's magicians, purveyors of joy, imaginers of the uncommon. They stir our pots; they ruffle our feathers. They paste twinkling stars on the dark night sky of life's drab dailiness. Living by magic, they let us recapture the magic in ourselves. Knowing that love is the only real magic there is, they invite us again—with their words, with their ways, with their dreams, with their faith—to believe in the magical power of love.

Today, let your heart be ribboned with thanks for a person whose magic has beautifully altered your life.

Holding the Vigil

*H*ow can we be loving to the person who is suffering, the friend who must go through the disfiguring surgical procedure, the colleague unfairly accused, the parent bowed down by the insults of infirmity? We can try as much as we can to enter the situation with them, with our presence, with our words, with presents and flowers as symbols of our love, our recognition of what they are going through.

But we need to remember that sometimes holding the vigil is all that is needed. Without fanfare we can quietly light a candle in our souls on behalf of the person who is suffering; we can open our hearts and transmit the healing power of our love.

Sleeping Dogs

*R*emember the old adage, let sleeping dogs lie? Sometimes it's just the right formula for love. What it means is don't make an issue out of everything. Not every single thing is worth fighting over, analyzing, or even working out.

If he didn't remember the whipped cream for the strawberries, don't make a federal case out of it. If she used up all the soap in the shower, don't nail her to the cross. We all make mistakes and for no particular or emotionally significant reason.

If you've been overreacting, cool it. Let the little things pass; save your energy for what's really important. There are more than enough really big things to argue about.

OCTOBER 29

Mythic Friendship

*B*eneath every friendship is the mythic image of the role that you fulfill for one another, a portrait of the real, healing meaning of your relationship.

Through this image you discover that a friend is a brother or sister in spirit, the father you never had, the mother who will never leave you, the magician who has the answer, or the image of yourself that you have been looking for for years.

To see our friends in this light is to extend the meaning of our relationships with them, to know that, beyond the simple sweet pleasures and interactions we share, something far more complex is going on.

Today take a look at the mythic portraits of your friends. Who are they really? What role do they play? What is the hidden history that you are healing through them?

Relationship: The Undertaking

*L*ove is an emotion, but a relationship is an undertaking. The degree to which we feel loved in our relationships has to do precisely with how we behave, what we say, offer, recognize, and respond to in another human being.

That's because, although we don't like to believe it, at the level of an interpersonal relationship love is contingent upon behavior. Love, the emotion, just doesn't stick around forever in the face of inattention or abuse on the part of the people involved.

Therefore, if you want your mate to feel the love you have in your heart, make it your business to listen, to discover what, at the level of her soul, she needs to hear, to see, to be shown, and to receive; what, at the depth of his soul, he needs to be told, how he needs to be touched, encouraged, cherished, believed in.

Someone Else's Silence

When someone close to you who is normally open and communicative suddenly withdraws, clams up, or gets silent, you may have a tendency to get critical or angry, to judge or attack. Changes in emotional behavior always mean something, and it takes compassion to keep from jumping to judgment, to try, instead, to understand.

So when someone close to you suddenly goes silent, rather than judging or abandoning them, very gently inquire, "Has something happened? Are you having a difficult time? Is there something you'd like to talk about?"

Step into someone's silence with loving words and they may step out of it with you.

Nurturing the Vividness

*L*ove is nurturing what is alive in another person. What is vital in each of us is vibrant and extraordinary. It may even, according to the conventions of our individual thinking, seem inappropriate or strange. But love recognizes uniqueness in all its myriad forms and knows that it is this vividness in each individual that is the spark of the divine.

Thus, we should always search for what is unique in the people we love and resist the temptation to reshape it according to our own precepts or desires. Instead, we should do everything we can to foster its fulfillment, to invite it to explode and expand.

Allowing the Other to Be

A lot of times, rather than simply being overjoyed by our relationships, we want to control them, smooth them out or nail them down, tailor them precisely to meet our own needs. Instead of allowing the person we love to have wings, we tie stones to his feet, ensuring that he will drag along beside us, going no faster than we are, headed for only the destinations that we have in mind.

When you find yourself dictating love, trying to contain it, behaving like a frantic Lilliputian endlessly trying to tie down the Gulliver of your dreams, you need to remember that real love means allowing the other to blossom, even if it isn't in precisely the ways that you intended or imagined. When you can offer this freedom, you're much more likely to receive it in return.

Anger as Self-Love

*A*nger is audible fiery prayer, the passionate plea through which we say that, although we have been loved badly in the past, we believe we deserve to be well loved now.

In expressing our anger we reveal our hopes; in speaking our anger, we reveal the inestimable value we place on our own souls. Anger is the emotion of assertion; when we communicate our anger we insist on our right to be treated well by those who profess to love us.

So honor your anger when it occurs. Is there something you're mad about? Something your sweetheart has done or forgotten to do? If so, try to find a creative way to express it so that instead of being a divisive explosion, your anger can be a call for more love.

A High Art

*L*istening well is one of the high arts of loving. In listening, suspending your own inner dialogue and self-involvement, you invite yourself into one of life's greatest mysteries, the experience of a wholly other, totally different human being.

Listening is a gift to your beloved, but it is also a present for yourself. For when you really listen to another person, you discover who they are. You see how they are both like you and unlike you—as much like you as your own reflection in a mirror, as different from you as a rare, almost extinct wild animal.

Listening gives you others. It also gives you yourself.

To Feel Love

Since we all need more love, it often seems that if only we could get more love we would feel more love.

The truth is that the experience of feeling love comes not just from having our own need for love fulfilled (he brought me a bouquet of flowers—therefore I feel loved), but from the more mature experience of being able to see ourselves as capable of giving the love (the beautiful words, the heartfelt empathy, the consoling touch) that another person needs.

Thus to feel love, *be* loving—and the rooms of your heart will be filled to overflowing.

Being and Feeling

*L*ove is both a state of being and an emotion. When we experience it as a state of consciousness, we are in harmony with all that is around us, with the world we inhabit, and the life in which we partake. We know we belong to the universe; we can be generous with our souls.

Love, the emotion, is an array of heart-dazzling feelings we have about another person. Love, the feeling, allows us to be happy, joyful, and optimistic. We feel attraction, connection, expectation, and hope.

While you may not always feel love, the emotion, you can always invite yourself into the presence of love as a state of being. The more you allow the former, the more you will experience the latter until, with time, no longer separate and parallel, they become one.

The Blindness of Love

*A*s we have been so often told, love, the great feeling we have at the outset of our romantic adventures, is blind. What this means is that we suspend the objective, judgmental, evaluating part of our perceptual capabilities and allow ourselves simply to feel.

However, life in real time is much more complex than feelings. We have obligations and responsibilities; we have circumstances and context. In addition to present feelings, we have to deal with feelings from the past that can crop up, unexpected and uninvited, and make havoc of our current emotions.

Because of this, it is at precisely the time and place in which blind love and concrete reality intersect that love asks the most of us. For while new love is truly and sweetly blind, reality is unbelievably demanding.

Moving toward Peace

I nvite yourself to move toward peace in your relation-ship by acknowledging to the person you love how deeply you long for peace. Ask her what single small change she would like you to make (not leaving the mail on the dining room table, not playing the television so loud, always kissing her good night, saying a prayer of thanksgiving for food on the table) in order to expand her sense of peace, of harmony in the life you share.

Then tell her what you would like her to do to make your union more serene—not leaving her cosmetics strewn all the bathroom counter, not screaming hysterically when her girlfriend shows up at the door. What can you do together to increase your domestic, emotional, and spiritual sense of harmony?

Peace is a state of grace, but it is created through effort, through the graciousness of knowing—and doing—the things that, in fact, create a sense of peace for one another.

Love Has No Boundaries

*T*hink of the peace you feel, the great sense of the true perfection of things, for example, after you've made love, after you've cried with a friend, after a moving conversation, after someone has wonderfully acknowledged you. All these are moments when we are blessed to have touched the limitlessness of love.

Love has no limits, no boundaries. Love erases our differences, and into love are we all dissolved. Love is at once larger and intricately smaller than anything we know. Love impales us and embraces us and chases us and takes us by surprise. Love is everything we know and everything we do not know; it is everything that, in the time that is no time, the place that is no place, we shall finally come to know.

NOVEMBER 10

Initiation Period

*E*very relationship, whether a marriage, a friendship, the relationship between a parent and a child, or a boss and an employee, goes through a period of initiation.

This is the time in which the relationship wobbles, seeking its footing, not knowing where it's going. This is a time of wonder and doubt, of feeling as though you are losing your way, of looking for landmarks that constantly seem to elude you, because only through initiation will they come into being.

Don't be alarmed if this is the emotional no-man's-land you find yourself in. It is in the very nature of initiation that there aren't any road maps. To be comforted, ask yourself what is being created here. A new relationship? The healing of a past hurt? A new power in yourself? Know that in time the discomfort of your initiation will become the measure of the quality of the relationship you have created.

The Good Fight

*I*n fighting, every sentence that moves toward healing and resolution, every ounce of confession, every admission of culpability, needs to be underlined by an expression of thanks and acknowledgement by the person who is listening. "Thanks for telling me; now I understand better why you said the thing that hurt me"; "I accept your apology; thanks for saying 'I'm sorry.'"

This is the choreography of honorable conflict: responding positively to every remark that moves, no matter how delicately, in the direction of healing and resolution. In adopting this as a general rule, you will transform the fighting in your relationship from conflict for conflict's sake to controversy whose most valuable outcome will be the wonderful strengthening of your union.

The Intelligence of Love

*L*ove requires intelligence, not only in the generosity of giving but also in the recognition of who it is that we are giving to, what he enjoys, what she rejoices in receiving.

That's because we all need love to be delivered to us in precisely the ways in which we are capable of receiving it. If your sweetheart is blind, you can't court her by sitting on the couch and watching videos. If your beloved is deaf, you can't woo him with Chopin and Rachmaninoff.

Just as the blind woman can receive the touch of your hand on her cheek but not the image from a photograph, or the deaf man can be moved by Picasso but not the Grateful Dead, so each of us has certain capacities to receive that are well developed, and other avenues to reception that are broken or underdeveloped.

What makes your beloved feel loved?

Total Freedom

*L*ove is the antithesis of ownership, dominance, and oppression. Therefore you will know you are in its presence when you feel yourself able to be most wonderfully all that you are.

The person who really loves you will have a sense, intrinsically, of who you are and will not only invite you to be most fully yourself, but through the miraculous transformations of love, will inspire you to become the most highly developed version of yourself.

When you feel pinched, downtrodden, and crunched, like a sparrow scrunched into a matchbox, you are not in the presence of love, but of someone's need to control you. When you are truly loved by another human being, you are free to be yourself. True love grants absolute freedom, the freedom to be engaged in the process of your own development.

Love Is the Glue

*T*oday, remember that love is the glue that can patch up your heart when you've been wounded by your sweetheart, when you've spoken harsh words to your child, when you've been unspeakably mean to your best friend.

Through love and with love, we can repair the bridge between us, the bridge that can lift us across the abyss created by miserable circumstances, our own impatience and fear, or seemingly overwhelming hard times.

We can't be perfect, and from time to time we will wound one another greatly. But with the glue of love we can cement our fractured relationships back together, remaking them into a fine mosaic, exquisite in color and form.

Love's Sonata

*T*he hallmark of a good relationship is that it is generally harmonious. Whatever other characteristics, flaws, or faults it may have, in its essence it is harmonious, at its core it possesses an intrinsic sense of just rightness.

This means that even in the midst of all the things that go awry in your relationship, even in the presence of all the things that you yourselves perpetrate upon it, you will come again and again to the still point at its center, the *basso continuo* against which the ever-altering melodies of your relationship will endlessly play themselves out.

So no matter how out of tune your relationship may seem at the moment, allow yourself to feel once again the resonance at its center. There is no more powerful thematic resolution than acknowledging the harmony of your individual instruments.

Self-Assertion

Self-assertion—knowing what you want and making a case for it in the presence of the person who loves you—is one of the hallmarks of a healthy self-love, one of the finest privileges of a vibrantly alive relationship.

This means that in times of conflict, rather than backing down, giving up, or shutting up, you will quietly but firmly state what you need and be willing to clarify or reiterate if the first time through you don't get the response you need.

If you're like most of us, there's probably something in your life that's bugging you about which you haven't asserted yourself. Today, stop and figure it out, then take the risk of having the conversation that will move you from the cowardice of hiding out to the boldness of healthy self-assertion.

The Magnitude of Love

*N*othing in your life is more important than the love you feel, need, or receive. No accomplishment however celebrated or remunerated can ever match it. No tragedy will ever utterly displace it; no adventure, no matter how grand or captivating, will ever equal its immense power in your life.

Love will be tougher than all the ridiculous and challenging demands of responsible adulthood, greater than all the heartrending sorrows and unredressed wounds of childhood, more powerful than the piddling disappointments of daily life. For love is bigger than sorrow and longer than time. Love is larger than life.

Invite Love In

*N*othing will teach your more about your emotional pain, your soul, your wounds, your dreams, your values, your longings, your weaknesses and strengths, than a day-to-day relationship with another human being.

Therefore, if you want to grow, if you want to be all that you might be or can be, invite a relationship into your life.

To invite a relationship into your life, believe that it can happen, get down on your knees and beg for it; and when it shows up take some risks: Reveal one thing you've been keeping to yourself (I've always been afraid). Ask one intimacy-exploring question (What's your secret dream?). Pay one real heartfelt compliment (You're beautiful).

Nothing will give you more of yourself, or bring you a greater sense of connection, than having "a relationship."

Gifted Parenting

When we see the innumerable bruised souls of children gone wrong in adulthood, we see that what so many parents call loving is not love at all but judgment, compression, restriction, competition, and spiritual annihilation. Our fears often make us draw the world small, and our fears for our children, rather than helping us to protect them, can make us close down their worlds and crumple their delicate spirits.

The truth is that we may not really be bigger or wiser than our children, and therefore our greatest wisdom ought to be to recognize that fact. Only very gifted or very loving parents allow their children to teach them. Strive to be one of them.

The Habits of Loving

*I*n every relationship there are particular ways in which you come together and share yourself with another human being, practices that are special for you both. This may be making love. It may be witty repartee after dinner. It may be walking on the beach every Sunday, working in the garden on weekends, kneeling in prayer, mourning together, throwing dinner parties, or lying side by side, skin to skin, every night when you sleep.

No matter how seemingly banal, ridiculous, odd, or ordinary they may seem, these habits, rituals, and happenings are precious. They are of inestimable value. For thereby are we nourished; therein do we love.

Love Holds the Mirror

*I*nside the intricacy of our psyches, we all know how much we need to be seen. None of us has come of age having been seen so well that we can truly see ourselves: who we are, how we look, what we came here to do, how we are broken, what moves and touches us.

Knowing the particular ways in which you need to be mirrored—and discovering the ways in which the person you love also needs to be given an image of him- or herself—is one of the kind undertakings of love.

Take a moment today to identify some aspect of yourself that is still invisible to you—your wit, your ability as an artist, your intelligence—and tell the person you love how very much you need this to be reflected back to you. Love is the mirror in which we are given back the truest image of ourselves. Ask for the mirror to be held for you; hold up the mirror for your beloved.

Making Love

*M*aking love is more than physical self-indulgence, more than physical relief. It is a dialogue between two souls, the interface of the material and spiritual.

If you are disappointed in your sexual relationship, ask yourself how your view of sex has limited the quality of your experience. And the next time you make love, allow yourself to enter into it not simply as a physical pleasure but as an encounter with the holy.

Too Much Love?

*T*here really is no such thing as loving your children too much. You can love them wrongly—stupidly, by not paying enough attention to who they are; selfishly, by training them to serve you; blindly, by overlooking their incredible uniqueness—but these are not forms of love but of parental ignorance.

Don't be afraid to love your children. Love them strongly, gladly, wisely: with your heart, with your arms, with your mind; with your affection, with your anger, with your truth; with the willingness to reveal yourself to them as a real and feeling human being.

Don't fall for the stingy old wives' notion that loving your children too much will "spoil" them, for the degree to which you love them is the degree to which they will be whole—the degree to which, in time, they will be able to give love in return.

Not a Free-for-All

*L*ove isn't a license for bad behavior. Just because you love someone doesn't mean you can't hurt them.

Making fun of your wife because she has poison oak, or your husband because he gained ten pounds, or your child because he fell in the mud, is not all right. It isn't true that "She's my wife; she doesn't mind," or, "He's my husband; it doesn't matter," or, "He's just a kid." It all hurts; it always matters; it always feels awful.

Be conscious today of what you say, think, and do so your behavior will truly—and always—be the embodiment of the good things you feel in your heart.

Listening with Your Heart

*R*eal love listens, knowing that it is in the mystery of exchange that we are bonded and that such an exchange occurs not only through what is said but though what is profoundly received. Speaking is done through the mouth but listening is done with the heart where meanings sink in like a stone in a pond, leaving an imprint at the deepest level.

Take the opportunity of this new day to really listen to someone. For while you may be relieved when you speak—delivered of the burden of information or feelings that you'd like to share—you will be transformed when you listen. The stone that falls to the bottom of the pond when you listen impinges on your soul, asks you to make room in your heart for the imprint of the essence of another human being.

In Union

*T*o love is to know that you live in union with all other creatures in a world that is itself alive and constantly becoming; in short, to live is to know that you exist in a world whose highest harmony is love.

Whatever experiences, conflicts, or disappointments beset you on this day—sharp words, a canceled lunch date, the urgent phone call that wasn't returned—try to remember that these events are happening on the minor level of life. At the highest level we are all connected; everything is perfect, everything is simultaneously of the utmost importance and doesn't matter at all, and there is a magnificent, huge, invisible reason for everything. We are all in union.

The Love We Need

We think the love we want is the love we need to get; but perhaps the best-kept secret about love is that our greatest need is for the love we need to give.

Being able to love and to have our love received is the greatest satisfaction love has to offer us; for in seeing ourselves as capable of loving, we unearth the purpose for our existence. We see in the profoundest of ways the meaning of our being, for we perceive ourselves most fully when we experience our capacity to love.

How have you cut off your own impulse to give? What compliments have you kept to yourself? What offerings, material or spiritual, have you been a little to shy to share? What do you have to give that you've been holding back? Give it today.

Offerings from the Angels

*I*n a certain way we are all impoverished beggars aching for the mothering and fathering we never got enough of. Therefore, when we are in a relationship, one of the major questions is how we are ever going to get nurtured. We want, we need; we are desperate, hungry, and cold, and our first concern, whether conscious or unconscious, is with our own immense menu of unmet needs.

Having our wounds tended, having our tears dried, being held at last in the sweet embrace that can dissolve our ancient sorrows—these all are the promises, the holy medicines of newfound love.

But binding wounds, wiping tears, becoming the arms whose embrace can alter the chemistry of the wounded soul—these are the miracles of love matured, love taken in, transmuted, and, as though an offering from the angels, returned a thousandfold.

Absolute Safety

*L*ove is opening with absolute safety. This means that rather than protecting ourselves—what we do, what we say—we trust that we are in an emotional environment that is truly a sanctuary for us, and that within it we can reveal what is deepest in our souls.

Although this process of opening is one of vulnerability and therefore scary, it is also the very experience that allows us to develop an exquisite closeness with the people we love. Opening ourselves in the presence of another is the love we can receive, and the granting of this opening to others is the love we can give.

Being Mirrored

*T*o be mirrored is to be given back an image of ourselves. When we are mirrored we come into possession of ourselves in a different, more powerful way. Rather than the somewhat stuttering unsureness we often feel from knowing ourselves from the inside, we are given an outside picture that allows us to perceive ourselves with a greater sense of conviction.

Allowing yourself to be mirrored is one of the signs of loving yourself. It means that you trust your own value enough to want people to show you yourself. It means that you want to be more—and better—than you have been in the past. It means that you're not afraid to see your beauty, your strength, or your flaws.

So allow yourself to be mirrored. Surround yourself with people whose essence can show you back to yourself.

Sexual Preference

*I*n making love as with everything else, your sweetheart isn't psychic. He or she needs to be told what you like and don't like. While sexual communication is often difficult, the starting point is what we already know about our fears, our sense of freedom or constriction, and our sensuality: "I love it when you touch my face"; "Please touch me very gently—it takes my body a while before it can receive what it's feeling."

In addition to communicating your preferences, you need to ask about the other person's: "Would you like the lights out? Am I going too fast?"

Although these things may seem strange—we never, for example, heard our parents say them—we do need to tell and show one another what we desire. For then our sexual encounters will be more than mere sex; they truly will be making love.

Problems Are Creative

We often bumble around in the slime pits of our lives, waiting, hoping, and praying for the day when things will settle down, when all our problems will be solved, and we can live in utmost bliss. But that day never comes—and fortunately so.

For in relationships as in life problems create change. Difficulty enlivens us, crisis moves us into change and change initiates transformation. We may not like problems, but they become the portals to the miracles by which we discover the mysteries in the person we love and the most profound truths in ourselves.

What do you see revealed to you when you think about the conflicts in your relationship in this way? How have you changed because of the problems you have encountered?

The Power of Reconciliation

W hen you can really love the person who has wounded you—with spontaneity, deep feeling, and genuine delight—then your own heart will have been healed of the wound, and you will be in the experience of reconciliation, an aspect of true love.

Reconciliation is more than repressing, forgetting, or rationalizing the hurt someone has inflicted on you. Reconciliation is turning around the pieces of the puzzle so you can see your "enemy" in a new light, so you can see him outside the context of the pain he has caused you—as a person trapped in his own context, suffering in his own right.

Who has hurt you that you would like to take back into your heart? How could you turn the puzzle around so you could see her differently, so that your heart could reopen?

Remembering Is Loving

*I*t is the looking glass of memory that binds us to the beauty of this life. When we remember the beautiful things—lightening bugs, the slam of the screen door on summer evenings, clean sheets, warm baths, the sound of voices in the living room, leaf fires in autumn, hot cocoa, sleigh rides—we are remembering and loving life.

Remembering is more than mere recollecting. It is honoring your incarnation, giving thanks for the gift of life.

The Responsibilities of Love

*L*ove is not only a feeling; it is also a practice. It is not only a miracle; it is also a discipline. It is not only a gift; it is also an undertaking.

To remember this is to partake of love at a different level and on different terms than usual, and not to be disgruntled when love requires effort or makes extraordinary demands.

Is there some responsibility of love that you have been shirking—a conversation you should have had with your wife or your son, a word of encouragement you were too tired to give to a friend, a position you needed to take in your community on behalf of your neighbors or friends?

The power of your love changes things. Today embrace the responsibilities of love, and honor yourself by knowing that you are sturdy enough to carry love's burdens.

The Communion of Response

*L*ove is response, the answering back with your body, your mind, your words, your kisses, your touches, and your looks to the joy, delight, anguish, heartache, good fortune, curiosity, achievement, disappointment, and exaltation of the person you love. Response is the echo of one soul to another, the endlessly outwardly rippling circles that what has been felt, said, done, or left undone by your beloved has been made real to you by your response.

Take note right now of how much or how little you respond to whom, and how much or how little you are being responded to.

Response is essential. Response is union.

Becoming Visible

O ne of the greatest emotional problems in this country is narcissism. So many of us can't see ourselves because no one has seen us and thus we can't see anyone else. We feel invisible and, unable to sense that we exist ourselves, we have a difficult time honoring the existence of another human being.

Seeing and loving yourself, therefore, is of the greatest importance. For without self-awareness, we can never love anyone else. However, self-awareness is an intricate task that involves a measure of focused self-attention.

Allow yourself to see yourself today. Look in the mirror and see your beautiful face. Then think about yourself, your personal style, your needs, your talents, and your dreams. Thinking about yourself is mental seeing and, rather than being the self-involved enterprise we often imagine it to be, it is a step on the journey toward compassion, the spiritual self-discipline that is the portal to really loving another human being.

Our Parents' Business

*N*o person is without a history or context. We are all living out the unfinished emotional legacies passed down to us by our parents. As conscious, discovering individuals we must live our way through all the things they have not resolved until, having come to the place where we have transformed their tragedies and our childhoods, we can finally emerge as ourselves.

What is your mother's unresolved problem? What is your father's unresolved issue? How have you taken on their unfinished business?

Starting today, give your parents' problems back to them by looking into your future and focusing on what you need to accomplish in your own life.

Love's a Spendthrift

O f real love, love that truly apprehends, willingly discovers, and generously responds, you can never give too much.

We sometimes do feel as though we give too much—time, attention, energy, money—but when we really love and are loved in return there's no such thing as keeping track.

Love's a spendthrift; it gives all and gets everything back.

To Serve Love

W e came here to serve love. Whatever you may think is the reason you came to earth, you have understood it only in part if you haven't understood that you came here to serve love.

Whatever we do, no matter how commonplace or pedestrian it may seem, at some level it is part of our contribution to the evolution of the human stream.

Serving love means that we are here to console one another, to be connected, to erase all the differences that divide us, and to remember that before and after all time, we are One.

Tell Your Story

*B*ehind every outburst and conflict in a relationship, behind whatever pushes your buttons, drives you up the wall or makes you crazy, there's a story at the center of which lies some hidden pain. Telling that story, sharing the pain you may want to conceal, plants seeds that can blossom into flowers of understanding.

So when conflict arises, look for your story and tell it, or allow the person you love to tell you his or her story. Stories enable us to meet one another at the level of our pain with the gift of our compassion.

What is the story, painful, embarrassing, poignantly revealing, that you need to tell? Let yourself think of the story today, and maybe tomorrow you'll have the courage to tell it to someone you love.

The Poison of Possessiveness

*I*n our antiquarian mythologies we all seem to think that at its core love has to do with possessiveness, that if we love someone, we will possess and be possessed by that person.

In fact, possessiveness is the antithesis of love. It treats a person like an object. It destroys autonomy. It eliminates freedom. It is a form of spiritual tyranny.

Except for sexual exclusivity, which is a gift and a conscious choice, no one belongs to anyone else. We all belong to ourselves, and the more we try to possess someone the less of them we will actually have to enjoy.

Temple of Transformation

*N*o relationship is perfect. No relationship ever offers everything you want and need.

In a good relationship, even a wonderful one, you get your *sine qua non*, the thing you absolutely cannot live without—emotional availability, passionate sexual bonding, endless fabulous conversation, spiritual union, athletic companionship—and some of the things you really want—flowers for your birthday, a trip to Aspen every winter, tolerance of your mother, strong arms to hold you, sweet hands to wipe way your tears. The rest is compromise.

The *sine qua non* is your humble homestead; the thing you really want is your vacation dream house, and the arena of compromise is the temple of your personal transformation.

To be realistic about the love you want and can get, make a list: What is your *sine qua non?* What are a few other things you'd be happy to receive? About what are you willing to compromise?

Say Thank You

S aying thank you creates love. It acknowledges that someone has loved you, that from the bounty of her spirit she has given something you need, that he has honored you with his clear perception of you.

Saying thank you expresses your appreciation to the person who has been so generous to you, but it is also, and perhaps more important, the way you allow yourself to be changed by the gift. Therefore, not saying thank you is a subtle form of not growing. It keeps you from experiencing the effect of what you have been given.

Who do you need to thank? For what? How have you changed because of what has been given to you?

Speaking the Truth

When we tell the truth we enter into a state of love with others. We honor them. We trust that they want to stand in the presence of the truth with us.

The truth we tell unites us with them and with some larger verity, reveals the deeper truth of the entire universe, and reminds us that truth can be known and that we ourselves can stand in alignment with it.

When we are in harmony with truth we are at peace on every level of our being, in our hearts, in our minds, in our cells, with every movement that we make.

Love is truth, and truth is love.

Beyond Conditions

*U*nconditional love is absolute acceptance. It is the love that apprehends the essence and embraces the eternal in the personal. This love sees beyond flaws and into possibilities, imagines the other in time beyond time, and apprehends the perfection in the imperfect individual.

Only unconditional love can make unspeakable demands. It can ask anything; for whatever it asks, it asks from the vantage point of already having seen the other person as perfect. It is devoid of the judgment, ridicule, criticism, pettiness, and impatience that make the requests of imperfect love feel like abuses and spirit-crunching demands.

Unconditional love reshapes the beloved in the form of love. Unconditional love begets unconditional love.

Really Taking Care

*T*oday make a list of all the things you would do if you started to really take care of yourself.

Include the things that you already do, the things that, instinctively or habitually, you have been doing for years. Then add some things you'd like to do, that you've often intended to do for yourself.

Make your list, then paste it up on your bathroom mirror or hide it in your underwear drawer, and do at least one new thing on the list today. Let yourself love yourself.

Learning Love's Ways

A great part of loving is becoming conscious of whom it is that you love, what it is that charms, enchants, and delights her, what nourishes his body and soul.

For no matter how precious or fine the thing you want to give may be to you, if it isn't equally valued by your beloved, it will be unable to be received. For it's only the love that we can actually take in that we experience as love, regardless of what the giver intends.

That's why so often people who profess their love with great passion don't get the response they want. They haven't found the recipe for delivering love in the most delicious form of the favorite dessert of the person they love.

What would delight your beloved? If you're not sure, ask. It isn't always the thought that counts. We feel loved when we get exactly what we need and want.

DECEMBER 19

Integrity, or Else

*U*ntruth, in whatever form, no matter how small or seemingly insignificant, disconnects us from the transcendent integrity the universe embodies and insists upon. Thus when we step out of truth, we step out of love.

That's why integrity—telling the truth, living up to your words, defining your personal morality and conducting your life according to it—is one of the finest attributes of love.

When we live in integrity, we are in harmony with the highest aspects of the cosmos. When we lie, cheat, hedge, fudge, defend, excuse, or rationalize, we devalue ourselves in the face of the larger truth of the All. By living our truth we live in love with the entire universe.

The Great Belonging

*H*aving a relationship places you in a very high state of being. It means that you are able to set aside your own self-centeredness and allow the complex reality of another human being—his history, his pain, her unique essence, her character—to blossom in your consciousness.

Allowing yourself to be invaded in this way is a spiritual act, for it means that you have broken the boundaries that keep you cocooned in your own self-absorption and allowed your ego to be penetrated in honor of the greater human belonging.

There is no finer thing we can do in this life. If you are lost in your fear of being overtaken by another human being, imagine yourself as a circle whose circumference has momentarily been opened, only to grow back together as a stronger circle, the circle of greater belonging.

The Castle of Your Soul

*T*he person who loves you will see you—not just how you look, but who you are inside, what makes you joyfully happy, what prickles your heart, what, in private, your dreams are made of.

Because the person who loves you sees you, you can reveal yourself even more. Because he sees your great kindness, you can show him the scars; because she sees your pure heart, you can show her the frailties you try to protect and obscure.

Seeing is receiving. To see another human being is to take him or her in completely, through the windows of your eyes, to the chambers of your heart and the castle of your soul.

Today, see if you can allow yourself to take in, ever so deeply, the beauty of one other human being.

Bad Fight/Good Joke

*I*f you're having a terrible fight and you don't know how you'll ever get through it, how about tossing in a good joke, a ridiculous red herring. Of course such a joke should be innocuous, not mean-spirited or poking fun at the other person, just something that will break the tension: "Honey, do you see the purple gorilla that's eating the geraniums?"

We can always get more steamed up or serious, be nastier and meaner. But do you really want to crush your sweetheart's spirit? A good fight comes to an end with no bodies bloody in the living room, so if you don't know how to go straight through the fight, why not step outside it for a minute?

Five Easy Pieces

Sometimes the simplest little questions can really enhance intimacy in your relationship. Try these:

What would you like me to give you?

What would you like me not to give?

What would you like me to receive from you in order to feel that I love you?

What would you like me to ask of you?

What would you like me to remember when we have grown old and the days of sweet music and dancing have come to an end?

The Real Fear

We are not afraid of love; we are afraid of all the places love will take us: old hurts, new lessons. To love is to revisit all the old painful places, and of course that's very scary. But to love is also to open ourselves to the possibility of healing our wounds, and to this invitation, no matter the fear that may accompany it, we should always respond.

Whether we are in an old relationship or a new one, we all have ways of protecting ourselves, of distancing so that we don't have to feel afraid. How can you be brave about love today? How can you put your fear on the shelf and invite more love into your life?

The Light That Falls

*L*ove is light, the huge mysterious power that enlivens not only our spirits but all of creation around us. The light that falls into our lives because we love and are loved is the light that will truly illumine us forever. It is the star we follow to stumble on magic, the moonlight of incredible romance and unbelievable passion, the sunlight of healing and growing, of spiritual well-being.

It is the light that enters our eyes when we behold the ones we adore, the light we create with our words, with the radiance of our spirits, with the whole beauty of our lives. Love is the light in which we live and breathe and love and dream. Love is the light that will fall on us, now and forevermore.

The Fear of Loss

*L*oving someone means living with risk, with the possibility of being abandoned. We can't control the risk, but by facing our fear of loss, we stand ever more ready to love and to be loved.

True love is bigger than our fears, more daring than our cowardice, more brave than all our limitations. True love steps over fear, allows change, invites expansion, explores the unknown. It's relatively easy to run, to protect, to separate, or withdraw—our challenge is to stay connected in spite of our fears.

When we find ourselves clinging to the other—Will he still love me tomorrow? Will she remain faithful tonight?—we should ask ourselves what we're really afraid of and try to express our fears. Then, instead of allowing our fears to take over, we can breathe in light, breathe out fear.

Not a Fantasy

We like to think of our relationships as the ultimate medicine bag, the tying up of all our loose ends, the fulfillment of all our dreams. In fact, love is not our dreams come true, but our reality invented.

What this means is that although magical things will happen—he may move, talk, or make love in exactly the way that you hoped for; she may look, walk, or embrace you in exactly the way you desired—there will also be all kinds of compromises and adjustments, things that aren't as you planned or imagined they would be.

In the midst of all the adjustments, though, lies the strand of your dream come true. Use it today to weave a new veil of magic around the two of you.

Love Is the Crucible

*L*ove is the crucible, the unmeltable changeless container in which we are tested by fire, melted down, and transformed. In love we are formed and reformed by the white heat of the unexpected revisitation of all the things in us that cry out to be healed: our shame and fear, our hurts and insecurities, our conflicts and our endless inner controversies.

Through our beloved we are once again brought face-to-face with what is unresolved in us. We meet again our father's absence or our brother's envy, our mother's cruelty or our sister's competition. We see our own childhoods mirrored in every direction. Through love we are invited to reenter them again but differently, to reexperience and grieve the losses of the past, and thus to redeem them.

Love's Creative Power

*I*t is love that fashions us into the fullness of our being—not our looks, not our work, not our wants, not our achievements, not our parents, not our status, not our dreams. These all are fodder and filler, the navigating fuels of our lives; but it is love: who we love, how we love, why we love, and that we love that ultimately shapes us.

It is love, before all and after all, in the beginning and the end, that creates us. Today, remembering this, let yourself take in the moments, events, and people who bring you, even momentarily, into a true experience of love. Then allow all the rest—the inescapable mundanities of life—like a cloud, to very quietly drift away.

Loving Our Children

*L*oving our children means honoring their identities, believing that they are individuals in the process of becoming, who have—among their many and sometimes frustrating attributes—talents and abilities that may exceed in scope and dimension the powers we ourselves possess.

Loving our children means that rather than squashing these miraculous gifts we will stand in reverence of them, and at such a distance as to give them air and light enough to blossom. In other words, as well as protecting our children by being their parents, we will trust them to become themselves.

What can you do, now and always, to encourage the blossoming of your children?

Love Is Change

*Y*ou know you are in love when you notice change, when the mysterious power that quickens your heart begins to inhabit your everyday life. Something softens in you and you begin to move in a slightly different direction: your face looks wiser or younger, there's a light in your eyes, something different in how you move, the way your hands take hold of things.

People notice. "You look different," they say, or, "You look wonderful," or, "What's happened to you?"

And you say back to them, "I've fallen in love," and inside you know you are changing. Because being in love changes everything.

INDEX

ABOUT THE AUTHOR

For more than twenty-five years, Daphne Rose Kingma has worked as a psychotherapist helping thousands of individuals and couples understand and improve their relationships. Dubbed the "Love Doctor" by the *San Francisco Chronicle*, Daphne has appeared as a relationship expert on nationally broadcast television programs including *Oprah!, Sally Jessy Raphael*, and *The Leeza Gibbons Show*. The bestselling author of several books, including *Coming Apart, True Love, The Nine Types of Lovers,* and *Weddings from the Heart,* she lives in Denver, Colorado.

To find out more about Daphne, visit her website at www.daphnekingma.com

TO OUR READERS

Conari Press publishes books on topics ranging from spirituality, personal growth, and relationships to women's issues, parenting, and social issues. Our mission is to publish quality books that will make a difference in people's lives—how we feel about ourselves and how we relate to one another. We value integrity, compassion, and receptivity, both in the books we publish and in the way we do business.

We donate our damaged books to nonprofit organizations, dedicate a portion of our proceeds from certain books to charitable causes, and continually look for new ways to use natural resources as wisely as possible.

Our readers are our most important resource, and we value your input, suggestions, and ideas about what you would like to see published. Please feel free to contact us, to request our latest book catalog, or to be added to our mailing list.

2550 Ninth Street, Suite 101
Berkeley, California 94710-2551
800-685-9595 • 510-649-7175
fax: 510-649-7190 • e-mail: conari@conari.com
www.conari.com